YOUR CIVICS ROADMAP

Passing the U.S. Citizenship Test with Confidence

LEVAN NATALISHVILI

Dedicated to Michael Piston and Baldwin (Bob) Maull, my mentors.

ISBN: 978-1-7350407-4-5

Disclaimer:

This book is designed to assist readers in understanding the process of becoming a United States citizen. While every effort has been made to ensure the accuracy and reliability of the information contained herein, laws, procedures, and requirements may change over time. Readers should verify all information with official U.S. government sources or qualified legal professionals before making decisions related to citizenship or immigration.

This publication is not affiliated with, endorsed by, or sponsored by the United States government, U.S. Citizenship and Immigration Services (USCIS), or any other government agency.

For official information, visit www.uscis.gov

CONTENTS

We the People of the United States, in Order to form a more perfect Union, establish Justice, insure domestic Tranquility, provide for the common defence, promote the general Welfare, and secure the Blessings of Liberty to ourselves and our Posterity, do ordain and establish this Constitution for the United States of America.

Article I

Section. 1. All legislative Powers herein granted shall be vested in a Congress of the United States, which shall consist of a Senate and House of Representatives.

Figure 1: U.S. Constitution, public domain, National Archives

NOTE TO READERS

This guide is based on publicly available information about the U.S. naturalization process and is intended for study support. Always check USCIS.gov for the most current questions, answers, officeholders, and requirements.

★ ★ ★ ★ ★

ABOUT THE AUTHOR

Levan Natalishvili is a naturalized U.S. citizen and an immigration attorney – as well as a former social worker – whose life's work has been to help others achieve the American dream. In *Your Civics Roadmap: Passing the U.S. Citizenship Test with Confidence*, he channels his personal journey and professional expertise into a comprehensive guide for people who want to become U.S. citizens. This new book is especially crafted for aspiring Americans preparing for the U.S. naturalization test, transforming what can be an intimidating process into an achievable milestone with the right knowledge and mindset.

Levan understands the challenges of the immigrant experience firsthand. He immigrated to the United States himself and eventually took the Oath of Allegiance to become a U.S. citizen, so he knows the dedication and perseverance it takes to reach that goal. Before he began practicing law, Levan worked in social services, assisting individuals from all walks of life and fostering a deep empathy for the hopes and struggles of those pursuing better lives. These early experiences gave him a profound appreciation for the journey of aspiring citizens and a personal desire to help others along that path.

In his legal career, that empathy is matched by expertise. Levan earned his law degree and has spent years as an immigration attorney guiding families and individuals through complex immigration and naturalization processes. As a fully qualified immigration lawyer and a proud naturalized American, he is in a unique position to guide others on the path to citizenship. He has witnessed every step of this journey – from preparing for the civics exam to attending clients' swearing-in ceremonies – and he knows exactly what applicants need to succeed.

In 2020, Levan authored *A Guide to Immigration Law of the United States of America*, in which shared his own immigration story and provided a step-by-step overview of pathways to visas, residency, and naturalization. That work, as well as his extensive experience in the field of immigration law, established him as an authoritative voice, and now *Your Civics Roadmap* builds on that foundation with a focused mission: to help prospective citizens confidently pass the U.S. citizenship test. This new guide zeroes in on the final step of becoming an American – mastering the civics and history knowledge for the naturalization exam – and it does so with clarity, warmth, and encouragement.

Throughout *Your Civics Roadmap*, Levan demystifies the civics test by breaking down American history, government structure, and civic principles into clear, digestible lessons. He also shares practical study tips and real-world examples drawn from his years of helping immigrants, all to ensure that readers feel informed and supported every step of the way. Levan's tone is professional yet uplifting, reflecting his genuine belief that with the right guidance and confidence, every aspiring citizen can succeed. By connecting his own journey to the journey of his readers, he inspires people not only to pass the citizenship test, but to embrace their new role as informed, confident American citizens.

★ ★ ★ ★ ★

THE PURPOSE OF THIS BOOK

Congratulations on wanting to become an American citizen!

The United States of America today has a culture rich in diversity. That is because it is a society made up of people from all over the world. Global citizens have brought together many different ways of thinking and behaving, combining cultures both ancient and young to create something new. The result of all that includes countless innovations, as well as the building of one of the strongest and most accomplished nations in history. Now you, too, can be part of that incredible society.

Becoming a U.S. citizen can be an exciting and challenging process. It begins with taking the U.S. Naturalization Test, as well as understanding the fundamental values that define the American spirit, so that you can quickly fit in and enjoy a productive and meaningful life in your new home.

This book takes you through all the possible questions you could be asked on the Naturalization Test and provides the answers you will need to pass. It also provides additional information to help you understand more than just the basic answers, giving you insight into important aspects of American life and history so that you can better understand your new country and get along with your fellow Americans. For example, throughout these pages you will explore the colonial era and discover why the first Europeans journeyed to America. You will learn about the nation's first attempt at self-government under the Articles of Confederation and understand why that early system was replaced. You will follow the drafting of the U.S. Constitution to see how it established a stronger foundation for the country. Finally, the book dives deep into the Bill of Rights—the first ten amendments—to explain the freedoms it guarantees, like the rights to free speech and religious liberty, and why those rights are so important to Americans.

Studying this rich history alongside the test questions will help you remember the answers better and truly understand the country's values. By learning not just what the answers are but why they matter, you will gain the knowledge and confidence to embrace your new role as an informed and confident new American.

The U.S. Naturalization Test

We currently use the 2025 version of the test. There are 128 questions to study for the test. You will be asked up to ten questions during your exam. You are required to get six answers correct, and the test ends as soon as you do so.

You can find a quick-reference list of questions and answers at the beginning of this book. Explanations and additional information follow.

Exemptions and Accommodations

The "65/20 exception" is a special consideration for U.S. naturalization applicants who are 65 or older and have been permanent residents for at least 20 years; they can take the civics test in their native language and are exempt from the English test. Other exceptions include: the 55/15 rule (age 55+ and 15+ years as a permanent resident) and medical disability exceptions, which can exempt applicants from both the

English and civics tests if they are unable to test due to a physical, developmental, or mental impairment.

During the test, a USCIS officer will ask 10 of the 20 starred questions from the 2025 version of the civics test. To pass, applicants must answer at least 6 questions correctly.

Good luck!

QUESTIONS 1-15: PRINCIPLES OF AMERICAN GOVERNMENT

The form of government in the United States is called a republic or a representative democracy.

This means that power belongs to citizens who vote on how things are done and what laws are made. In a basic democracy, everyone would vote directly on every issue. For small groups or groups that do not vote often, that is a good system. But in modern times, with nations of millions of people, that is not practical. There are too many issues and too many laws, and most people have too much work to do to spend all day thinking about what laws to make.

In a republic or representative democracy, the public does not vote directly on what laws are passed. There is an extra stage between law creation and public vote. Citizens elect government representatives to vote for them and their interests. Voters trust their representative to do the right thing and to accurately vote the way their district wants them to.

The U.S. Constitution is the supreme law under which everything falls, and defines the parts and powers of the government. The nation is made up of many states united together under a central government, a system called a federation. This makes the U.S. a constitution-based federal republic.

Federalism

In the United States, the government is arranged so that multiple levels of government control the same territory. The overarching national government addresses issues that apply to everyone while states and local governments address regional concerns. All entities can make laws and operate independently from each other.

The United States has two levels of government: federal and state. The federal government is led by the President and Congress. Congress makes federal laws. Each state has its own government led by a governor and a state legislature. Powers not given to the federal government belong to the states or the people.

The federal government can influence states. One way to do this is through federal grants and federal aid. States receive federal money, but the contributions often come with requirements. Certain federal donations can only be used for specific purposes. For example, the National Minimum Drinking Age Act of 1984 says that states can only get funding for federal highways if they have a minimum drinking age of twenty-one.

In a federal system, power is spread out rather than concentrated in one person or group, as it is with a monarchy or dictatorship. This helps prevent abuse of power and limits corruption.

In a federal system, diverse groups are better represented in government. In America, the population of each state can directly petition their state regarding laws and policies. The same can be done on a municipal (city/town) level. These smaller levels of government counter the power of the national government and ensure that the national level pays attention to the concerns of everyone.

1. What is the form of government of the United States?

- *Republic*
- *Constitution-based federal republic*
- *Representative democracy*

Republic

People choose leaders in elections. There is no king or queen.

Constitution-Based Federal Republic

The country has two levels of government: national and state. The Constitution explains how power is shared. Leaders are elected.

Representative Democracy

People vote for representatives. Those representatives make laws and can be voted out if people are not happy.

2. What is the supreme law of the land? *

- *(U.S) Constitution*

In 1776, colonial rule was overturned, and self-government was achieved. Americans wanted a proper constitution for their new nation.

The Articles of Confederation, the United States of America's first Constitution, was adopted by all thirteen states on November 15, 1777. The ratification of all thirteen states occurred in 1781. However, this document was limited and not effective enough. Therefore, the nation's founders decided a new document was needed and began work on one.

The Constitution of the United States replaced the Articles of Confederation and was implemented on March 4, 1789. It is now the supreme law of the U.S.A.

What do the Articles of Confederation say?

The document created *before* the Constitution is the Articles of Confederation. The document's thirteen articles say the following:

1. The name of the combined thirteen states is The United States of America.

2. States remain sovereign entities, except where powers are specifically granted to the Confederation government.

3. The purpose of confederation is for states to enter into formal cooperation for common defense, the security of liberties, and their mutual and general welfare. They are bound to assist each other against all forces.

4. They establish equal treatment and freedom of movement between states, except for paupers, vagabonds, and fugitives from justice. Anyone who commits a crime and flees to another state will be extradited to the state in which they committed the offence.

5. They create the Congress of Confederation. Each state gets one vote and can send two to seven people to participate in the Congress. Congressmen may serve a maximum of three out of six years.

6. Only the Confederation government can conduct international relations or declare war. No state official can accept foreign gifts or foreign titles. In addition, each state had to train its own militia but cannot have a standing army.

7. Each state had its own military leaders for the rank of colonel and below.

8. States must raise money to give to the central government.

9. War and peace, the appointment of ambassadors, treaties and alliances, dealing with piracy, and weights and measures are solely the Confederation government's responsibility. Congress regulates post offices, regulates the military, and regulates the

armed forces. Congress cannot declare war or enter treaties/alliances, appropriate money, or appoint a Commander in Chief unless they have the agreement of nine or more states.

10. When Congress is not in session, a committee of nine or more states can execute its powers.
11. Canada may join the Confederation.
12. The Confederation will honor all debts contracted before the Articles of Confederation.
13. The Articles of Confederation are forever and can only be changed if all thirteen states agree.

Problems with the Articles of Confederation

The Articles of Confederation created a weak central government. Those who created the document were very concerned that the central government should not become too powerful, but in giving it too many boundaries, they failed to make it powerful enough.

Some problems with the Articles included the following:

- Each state had only one vote, no matter how large their population, so national votes did not accurately represent the population. A state with few people had the same power as a state with many people.
- Nine out of thirteen states had to approve a measure for it to pass, which was high.
- Amending an article required all thirteen states to vote for the change.
- Only states could levy taxes, and the central government had to request money from them. Therefore, the national government was often underfunded and could not pay debts or secure new funds.
- The central government had almost no military power and no way of regulating commerce.

The need for a stronger federal government eventually became apparent and led to the Constitutional Convention in 1787, where people discussed reforms (amendments) to the Articles of Confederation.

Figure 2: © Shutterstock / Ruslan Lytvyn used under license

Issues Addressed in the Creation of the Constitution

One can only imagine the long, heated discussions during the Constitutional Convention. There were discussions about slavery, representation, and the rights and powers of each state in relation to the government. After a while, it became clear that there were specific issues that delegates from the various states did not agree upon.

REPRESENTATION

Small states said that each state should be equally represented in government. In contrast, the states with more people upheld the idea of the Virginia Plan, that representation should be calculated according to the population of each state.

In the end, a compromise was reached. A legislature with two Houses was created, with a Senate where all states are equally represented, and a House of Representatives in which representations are appointed based on a state's free population plus part of the slave population.

SLAVERY

Slaves were not seen as people in those days. After some heated discussions, it was decided that only three out of every five slaves would be counted as people for representation in Congress. This became known as the Three-Fifths Compromise. The southern states had to agree that they would not import more slaves after 1808.

WHO COULD ELECT THE PRESIDENT?

The Electoral College is how the United States chooses the president and vice president. It was created in 1787 as a middle ground between letting Congress decide and having everyone vote directly. The Electoral College is not just one group; it is a process. Today, there are 538 electors. A candidate must receive more than half of the electoral votes to become president. This means they need at least 270 votes.

Each state has a number of electors equal to its U.S. representatives and its two U.S. Senators. The electors give one vote for president and a different vote for vice president. This rule comes from the Twelfth Amendment.

In the first presidential election, held in 1788–1789, the electors chose George Washington as the nation's first president. He was elected by every elector, meaning he got all the votes.

COMMERCE

At that time, each of the U.S. states had their own ways of making money. In many ways, they were competing against each other. Therefore, it was decided that it would be in the best interest of America and its whole population if the economy was nationalized.

STATE POWER VS. FEDERAL POWER

Distinctions between central government and state power were debated and set out.

The central government would be responsible for the military and its maintenance, declaring war, setting standards (for weighing and measurements), and protecting copyrights and patents.

States would have power over their local government and education.

Some powers could be shared: collecting taxes, regulating interstate commerce, punishing criminals, and establishing courts.

In the end, the Virginia Plan and the New Jersey Plan were combined in a plan that became known as the Great Compromise or the Connecticut Plan. This describes Congress as we know it today.

Summary of the Articles of the Constitution

1. Defines Congress, the legislative branch of government (Senate and House of Representatives).
2. Defines the office, qualifications, and duties of the executive branch (President of the U.S.A).
3. Defines the judicial branch of government, including the court system and the Supreme Court.
4. Defines relations between states and between the states and the federal government.
5. Defines the amendment process so changes can be made to the Constitution.
6. Defines federal powers, including the Supremacy Clause.
7. Defines ratification of the Constitution with a majority of nine of the original thirteen states.

Signing the Constitution and Ratification

The Constitution was signed on September 17, 1787 by thirty-nine of the fifty-five attending delegates.

To be binding, the Constitution needed to be ratified by at least nine of the thirteen states. This way, the national Constitution would rest entirely on popular authority.

Delaware was the first state to ratify the new Constitution. The new Constitution took effect on March 4, 1789.

3. Name one thing the U.S. Constitution does.

- *Forms the government*
- *Defines powers of government*
- *Defines the parts of government*
- *Protects the rights of the people*

The Constitution of the U.S.A is the oldest and longest-standing written and codified national constitution still in use in the world. The Constitution consists of the preamble, seven articles that set out the national framework of national government, as well as twenty-seven amendments.

SETS UP THE GOVERNMENT

The Constitution was established to form the federal government and create a federal republic.

DEFINES THE GOVERNMENT

The Supremacy Clause states that the Constitution is the supreme law of the U.S.A. Any federal laws and treaties made under its authority constitute the "supreme law of the land" and take precedence over state laws.

The Constitution describes the rights and responsibilities of states and their relationship to the federal government, as well as the process of constitutional amendment.

There are three branches of government and a separation of their powers: legislative (makes the laws), judicial (adjudicates the laws), and executive (executes the laws). This is so that one branch cannot become too powerful; it is a system of checks and balances.

PROTECTS THE BASIC RIGHTS OF AMERICANS

The Constitution protects the fundamental rights of all Americans. No one is above the law, and everyone, from citizens to leaders in the highest office, must obey.

The Constitution also provides for limitations to be placed upon the powers of the government to protect the fundamental rights of every citizen. America's main aim is to serve the citizens. In his Gettysburg Address Speech of 1863, President Abraham Lincoln said:

> *That these dead shall not have died in vain—that this nation, under God, shall have a new birth of freedom—and that government of the people, by the people, for the people, shall not perish from the earth.*

4. The U.S. Constitution starts with the words "We the People." What does "We the People" mean?

- *Self-government*
- *Popular sovereignty*
- *Consent of the governed*
- *People should govern themselves*
- *(Example of) social contract*

> *We the People of the United States, in Order to form a more perfect Union, establish Justice, insure domestic*

> *Tranquility, provide for the common Defence, promote the general Welfare, and secure the Blessings of Liberty to ourselves and our Posterity, do ordain and establish this Constitution for the United States of America.*

We the People, the opening statement to the U.S. Constitution, has been referred to as the three most important words in the history of American democracy. People (citizens) empower the government of the U.S., and without the people, the Constitution would not have an impact on the government of the United States, making it a *fundamental law of the land.*

When first drafted, there was no mention of We *the People of the United States.* It read, *We the United States,* followed by a list of the states. The wording was changed because a value had changed. America very much values the opinions of its citizens. The Founding Fathers established the Constitution to adhere to the wants and needs of the *people.* It contains a powerful message: America is owned by the people and not by the government. Democracy (popular sovereignty) is paramount to self-government. The founders specifically wanted to prevent America from becoming like nations in Europe, where all-powerful monarchs could do whatever they wanted and the upper classes controlled all the wealth and power. In America, wealth and power were meant to be shared.

In order to pass laws in America, those in positions of power require the consent of the governed. The people should govern themselves and not be oppressed by rulers, such as kings, dictators, and other tyrants.

The Constitution is an example of a social contract. This is an agreement between people that usually defines the legitimacy of government over citizens. Here, people willingly submit to the authority of the government in exchange for protection and rights.

Although placed in the Constitution only during the last days of the Constitutional Convention, the preamble contains the fundamental purpose and principles that the constitution is based on.

Some believe the preamble to be the enacting clause of the Constitution. However, it is essential to remember that the preamble itself does not assign any powers to the government or place any limitations on it. It does not have any legal power, but it has been used by the courts to interpret the meaning of various sections of the Constitution.

Purposes of the Constitution

FORM A MORE PERFECT UNION

When the Articles of Confederation were not sufficient anymore, there was a need for an improved government to better govern the people. So, the Constitution came into being.

The Constitution helps to keep the country together as one entity, especially during a crisis of war or any other circumstance that may occur, while using a system of checks and balances that help limit abuse of power.

ESTABLISH JUSTICE

All citizens must be treated fairly and have equal rights, regardless of their religion, skin color, or other individual differences. There must be laws, ways to enforce them, as well as fair punishments. The Constitution is a mechanism to remove corrupt people who break the law. No one is above the law.

ENSURE DOMESTIC TRANQUILITY

The framers of the Constitution wanted peace at home in America. This phrase was meant to prevent states from fighting each other and to deter violent rebellion. Today, domestic tranquility refers to maintaining political stability and protects and encourages peaceful demonstrations and assemblies.

PROVIDE FOR THE COMMON DEFENSE

The whole of America should stand together in times of adversity and times of military need.

PROMOTE THE GENERAL WELFARE

Public institutions, such as post offices, hospitals, and highway systems are a constitutional application of this general welfare clause in the Constitution.

SECURE THE BLESSINGS OF LIBERTY

The Constitution protects citizens from unjust laws and provides them with freedom from a tyrannical government.

5. How are changes made to the U.S. Constitution?

- *Amendments*
- *The amendment process*

An amendment is a change or an addition. Since 1789, the Constitution has been amended, or changed, only twenty-seven times. Article V of the Constitution details how amendments are made. The two-step amendment process includes a proposal, then ratification.

Amendments are proposed in Congress. They require a two-thirds majority in the Senate and in the House in order for the proposal to be sent to the states.

Amendments are ratified when three-fourths of state legislatures accept them.

Did You Know?

Changing the Constitution is extremely difficult. In more than two hundred years, over 11,000 proposals to amend the Constitution have been proposed in Congress, but only twenty-seven changes have been ratified.

6. What does the Bill of Rights protect?

- *(The basic) rights of Americans*
- *(The basic) rights of people living in the United States*

The Bill of Rights

When the Constitution was created, some of the states were highly concerned about freedom and protecting the individual rights of Americans. They felt that the federal government would have too much power. These people became known as the Anti-Federalists.

During the Philadelphia Convention in 1787 while others were busy signing the newly drafted Constitution, three delegates (George Mason, Edmund Randolph, and Elbridge Gerry) refused to sign. They felt that the Constitution should also make a provision for the protection of individual rights and that it must contain a declaration of human rights.

George Mason was quite adamant. He said: "I would sooner chop off my right hand than sign the Constitution without a Bill of Rights."

In the end, the Anti-Federalists insisted that omitting a Bill of Rights would be a massive flaw in the newly drafted Constitution. Therefore, they said they would sign the Constitution only on the condition that a Bill of Rights was added.

George Mason and Thomas Jefferson's influence led to the draft of the Bill of Rights, the first ten amendments of the Constitution. These were proposed and drafted by James Madison and played a huge part in the creation of the Constitution.

The first ten amendments of the Constitution are collectively known as the Bill of Rights. The Bill sets out each American civilian's guaranteed and fundamental rights and liberties, including the right to freedom of speech, freedom of religion, the right to due process by law, and the right to a speedy trial.

The Bill of Rights became part of the Constitution in 1791.

Who Drafted the Bill of Rights?

Figure 3: © Shutterstock / Ntguilty, used under license

James Madison (also a drafter of the Constitution) was tasked with drafting the Bill of Rights. He drew his inspiration from the Virginia Declaration of Rights (drafted by George Mason) and other political documents. Initially, he proposed nineteen amendments, which were narrowed down to seventeen by the House of Representatives and later narrowed down further to twelve amendments by the Senate. Eventually, ten amendments were ratified, and on December 15, 1791, the Bill of Rights became part of the United States Constitution.

7. How many amendments does the U.S. Constitution have? *

- *Twenty-seven (27)*

List of Amendments

1. Protects freedom of religion, speech, press, and assembly, as well as the right to petition the government.
2. Protects the right to bear arms (weapons).
3. Restricts housing soldiers in private homes.
4. Prohibits unreasonable searches and seizures and sets requirements for search warrants and probable cause.
5. Defines rules for indictment by grand jury, due process, self-incrimination, and double jeopardy. Protects the right to a speedy trial, notification of criminal accusations, confront your accuser, obtain witnesses, and retain counsel.

6. Protects the right to a jury trial and civil lawsuits.
7. Prohibits excessive fines and bail. Prohibits cruel and unusual punishment.
8. Says that rights not listed in the Constitution are still retained by the people.
9. Says the federal government has the powers only exactly detailed in the Constitution and all other powers belong to the states.
10. States cannot be sued by people outside the state.
11. The vice president is now elected together with the president instead of being the runner up in the election.
12. Abolishes slavery and involuntary servitude, except as punishment for a crime.
13. Defines citizenship, privileges and immunities, due process, and equal protection.
14. Prohibits denying someone the right to vote based on race, color, previous condition, or servitude.
15. Allows Congress to create an income tax without sharing the income with states.
16. Says senators are now elected by popular vote.
17. Prohibits making alcohol, *repealed with the Twenty-First Amendment.*
18. Gives women the right to vote.
19. Sets new dates for the start of Presidential and Congressional terms—January 20th for the President and January 3rd for Congress.
20. Repeals the Eighteenth Amendment.
21. Limits the number of times a person can be elected President.
22. Includes the District of Columbia in the electoral college.

23. Says you cannot take away someone's right to vote if they do not pay poll taxes.

24. The 25th Amendment to the U.S. Constitution deals with presidential succession and disability, establishes that the vice president becomes president if the president dies, resigns, or is removed from office.

25. Sets the voting age at eighteen years of age.

26. Laws that affect congresspersons salaries take effect after the next election of representatives.

8. Why is the Declaration of Independence important?

- *It says America is free from British control.*
- *It says all people are created equal.*
- *It identifies inherent rights.*
- *It identifies individual freedoms.*

The Declaration of Independence states that America was now free of British control. The thirteen colonies were now self-governing and at war with the British Empire. The Declaration was designed to be a political document and a statement of governing identity to the rest of the world. The document states that all people are created equal, and the Declaration identifies inherent rights and individual freedoms.

The Declaration of Independence states:

> *"We hold these truths to be self-evident, that all men are created equal, that they are endowed by their Creator with certain unalienable Rights and that among these are Life, Liberty and the pursuit of Happiness."*

The Declaration of Independence justifies why colonists of the original thirteen colonies wanted to rebel against Britain. It lists twenty-seven grievances against King George III and explains how he failed to protect their rights.

The Declaration says that all people have natural rights and that it is the duty of government to protect these rights. Should the government fail to do so, a new government should be put in place. Because the British government failed the colonists, Americans would now create their own government. The Declaration of Independence freed the American people from Britain.

Figure 4: © Shutterstock / Rawpixel.com, used under license

Fifty-six men signed the declaration. John Hancock, who was the president of the Continental Congress at that time, signed first.

9. What founding document said the American colonies were free from Britain?

- *Declaration of Independence*

10. Name two important ideas from the Declaration of Independence and the U.S. Constitution.

- *Equality*
- *Liberty*
- *Social contract*
- *Natural rights*
- *Limited government*
- *Self-government*

Important Ideas from the Declaration of Independence

EQUALITY

All humans are born equal. This does not mean they should have the same education, the same amount of money, or the same number of materials over the course of their lives. It means they should be treated as equals in terms of governing, the law, and fair treatment in society.

Achieving equality is constantly a work in progress. Over the history of the U.S.A, there have always been various kinds of discrimination. However, a great deal of progress has been made, significantly reducing discrimination based on gender, skin color, religion, sexual orientation, and more.

LIFE

In tyrannical governments, leaders can freely execute citizens. They might decide to kill an opponent or someone who questions their methods, or for any other reason. They can conscript citizens into armies and throw them into deadly wars without good reason.

The founders argued that we have a natural, untouchable right to life; that the government cannot kill people or send them to their deaths on a whim. It also means that it is the government's responsibility to provide the people with a good quality of life on an ongoing basis. That can mean providing clean water, education, health care, and public safety.

LIBERTY

Liberty refers to freedom from abusive power, the kind wielded by all-powerful monarchs, dictators, and other bad rulers. Liberty means having a voice in how the country is operated, including its laws and structures, and having the ability to pursue your own goals as long as they do not hurt others.

PURSUIT OF HAPPINESS

To pursue means to chase, but the founders originally meant this phrase to also mean to obtain happiness, so that people may practice and experience it. You do not just get the right to chase happiness: you also have the right to obtain it.

SOCIAL CONTRACT

The Declaration of Independence, like the Constitution, is a social contract. A social contract is an agreement between people, where they voluntarily submit to an agreed-upon government. We exchange some individual power for collective protection.

NATURAL RIGHTS

Natural rights are those that we are all entitled to simply by existing. They cannot be taken away.

Note that life, liberty, and the pursuit of happiness are only examples of natural rights and that more can exist.

SELF-GOVERNMENT

Government is established by the people and for the people. Government is a product of everyone (democracy), not something held by a few powerful people (e.g., monarchy, oligarchy, or dictatorship).

Did You Know?

The phrase *life, liberty, and the pursuit of happiness* is also found in the constitutions of Japan (1947) and South Korea (1987). It is also included in Ho Chi Minh's 1945 Declaration of Independence from the Democratic Republic of Vietnam.

The Canadian Charter of Rights includes the similar phrase *life, liberty, security of the person.*

11. The words "Life, Liberty, and the pursuit of Happiness" are in what founding document?

- *Declaration of Independence*

12. What is the economic system of the United States?*

- *Capitalism*
- *Free market economy*

Capitalism

Capitalism is an economic system in which property and businesses are privately owned and operated for profit, rather than owned by the government.

Characteristics include: private property, private accumulation of wealth, competitive markets, self-interest, profit-motive, economic freedom, credit and debt, wage labor, commodification, and more. Innovation and constant economic growth are strongly pursued.

Market Economy

In a market economy, prices of goods and services are determined by supply and demand, ideally without the intervention of government. America does not have a pure free market economy because the government does intervene with prices, to a degree, using taxes and regulations.

Criticisms of Capitalism

There are positive and negative points to most economic systems. Capitalism allows a wide degree of personal freedom when it comes to choosing where you work, establishing new businesses, innovating, and growing without unfair limitations. It is important that people own the means of production to ensure their liberty. If the government controlled all workplaces, citizens might not have a voice in how the economy operates and what kind of work they do. They would be unable to innovate on their own.

However, there are very significant negative points. Capitalism naturally exploits people. Because it fosters massive economic inequality, with wealth increasingly concentrated in the hands of only a few people, it is not sustainable. That wealth inequality directly weakens the natural rights enshrined in the Constitution and in the Bill of Rights. Some contend that a system of wealth inequality and rising debts has led to widespread manipulation and "wage slavery," which undermines individual freedoms.

Because of the drive to constantly increase profits rather than satisfy people's needs, a lot of labor and production are misdirected and wasted. We make money for the sake of making money rather than dedicating ourselves to goals that would benefit the most people. Wealth ends up in the hands of only a few individuals, and it becomes increasingly difficult to fund public works, such as maintaining infrastructure, funding education and health care, and preserving the integrity of a democratic government. A few get richer while most become poorer, so that most people have less liberty. Kings are replaced by billionaires, which creates many of the same types of problems.

Capitalism and the free market are somewhat restrained by taxes and regulations including a minimum wage, a limit to work hours, unemployment insurance, and laws against the sale of harmful goods (like certain drugs and weapons). However, the U.S.A faces many struggles as a result of its economic system, and the economy continues to be one of the most important issues for voters.

13. What is the "Rule of Law"?

- *Everyone must follow the law*
- *Leaders must obey the law*
- *Government must obey the law*
- *No one is above the law*

Rule of law is an ideal that says that everyone must follow the law. That includes leaders and those in government. No one is above the law. All government officers in the U.S.A pledge to uphold the Constitution, including the president and the justices of the Supreme Court.

However, some people argue that the ideal of the rule of law has eroded over time for those in power. All three branches of government have some flexibility regarding the law within the framework of the Constitution.

14. Many documents influenced the U.S. Constitution. Name one.

- *Declaration of Independence – see page 106*
- *Articles of Confederation – see page 29*
- *Federalist Papers – see page 115*
- *Anti-Federalist Papers – see page 115*

- *Virginia Declaration of Rights – see page 111*
- *Fundamental Orders of Connecticut – see page 111*
- *Mayflower Compact – see page 112*
- *Iroquois Great Law of Peace – see page 113*

15. There are three branches of government. Why?

- *So one part does not become too powerful*
- *Checks and balances*
- *Separation of powers*

The Three Branches of Government

In the past, most people lived in monarchies and other types of dictatorships where the government had all the power, and most of it was in the hands of one person. That meant the public had no voice and that the leader could do anything. This often led to abuse and suffering.

The founders of America wanted to create a country where that would not happen. They wanted a government that served and protected the people.

The three branches of the U.S. government are the legislative (Congress: the Senate, and the House of Representatives), the executive (President), and judicial (Supreme Court).

The government is divided into three branches of government power so one part does not become too powerful. The system of checks and balances ensures the separation of powers.

Congress makes laws, but the President can veto them and stop them. If a law does not adhere to the Constitution, the Supreme Court can strike it down.

The president appoints people to be the heads of various federal agencies, but Congress has the power to confirm or reject these people. Congress can also remove the president from office in exceptional circumstances. The Supreme Court can stop the president from actions that are outside the scope of the Constitution.

The president nominates people to the Supreme Court, and these people are confirmed by the Senate. The president can create executive actions, and Congress creates laws, but the Supreme Court can overturn both if it finds them unconstitutional.

QUESTIONS 16-62: SYSTEM OF GOVERNMENT

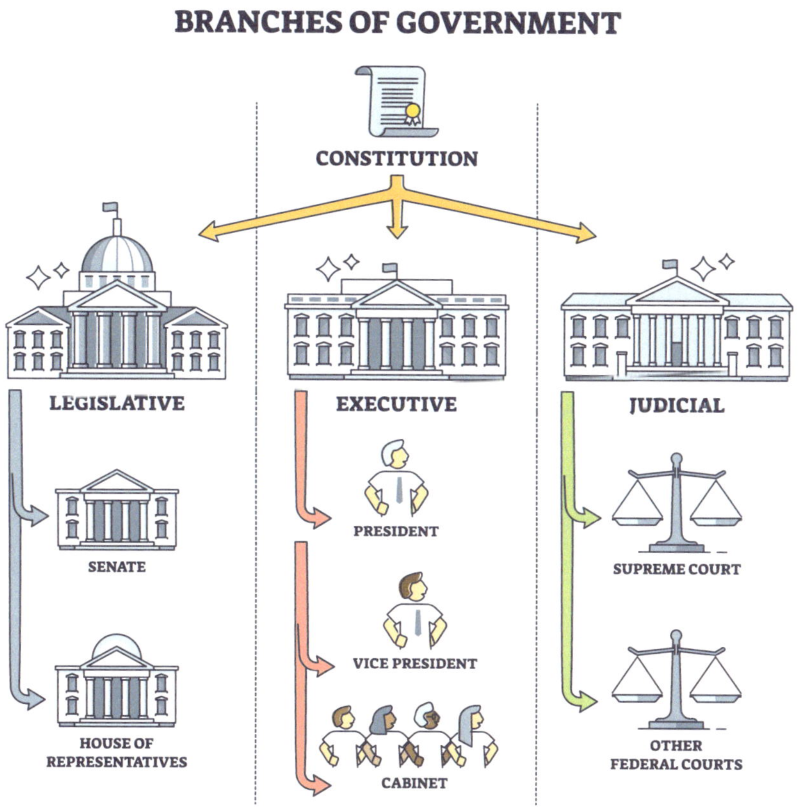

Figure 5: © Shutterstock / VectorMine, used under license

16. Name the three branches of government.

- *Congress*
- *Legislative*
- *President*
- *Executive*
- *The courts*
- *Judicial*

CONGRESS (LEGISLATIVE)

This branch of government makes laws. The people vote for representatives, who are expected to learn as much as they can about proposed laws and how they will affect people and then vote on whether to create or remove laws based on the will of voters.

PRESIDENT (EXECUTIVE)

This branch of government executes laws. That is, it oversees the machinery of government. Many agencies carry out government operations, such as the Department of Transportation and immigration agencies within the Department of Homeland Security.

THE COURTS (JUDICIAL)

This branch of government adjudicates laws. If someone is accused of breaking a law, judges analyze the accused's actions and decide if they have, and if so, how they are to be punished.

If someone questions the validity of a law, the Supreme Court can decide whether that law is valid according to the Constitution.

17. The President of the United States is in charge of which branch of government?

- *Executive branch*

The president is the head of state (ceremonial functions) and the head of government (Chief Executive). The president is Commander in Chief of the armed forces, receives ambassadors and other foreign dignitaries, can grant reprieves and pardons for federal offences against the U.S.A (except in cases of impeachment), has a great deal of influence in deciding policy in the government, and is usually the leader of their political party.

18. What part of the federal government writes laws?

- *(U.S.) Congress*
- *(U.S. or national) legislature*
- *Legislative branch*

Congress

The U.S. Congress (national legislature) is divided into two institutions: The House of Representatives and the Senate. Both Houses have equal power but different roles within the federal government. The thinking behind the system was to balance the interests of larger and smaller states.

Each state has an equal say in the Senate, regardless of population, and has two senators. In the House of Representatives, representation is based on the size of the state's population. For example, a small state like Vermont has only one representative in the House, whereas California has fifty-three.

Congress makes the federal laws of the United States of America.

Members of Congress

Members of Congress represent the people in their district. Congress members hold hearings, and they develop and vote on new legislation. All new bills must work their way through Congress before being signed into law by the president.

Congress works on a committee system to address issues. Committee members are people interested in the issue. The House has twenty standing committees, and the Senate has twenty permanent committees. A Congressperson might meet with various people to find out their ideas about different topics.

Senate members must be at least thirty years old, whereas the age minimum for the House of Representatives is twenty-five. All of these people must live in the state they represent, although it is not a requirement for members of the House to live in the district they serve.

Operations

The House has four times more members, so it is understandable that its operation must be more controlled. For instance, in the House, debate times are limited to one hour, whereas discussions in the Senate are unlimited by time. There are many more members in the House, so there is simply not enough time for everyone to have their say. In the Senate, because there is no limit on arguing a bill, Senators can employ the filibuster, which is arguing forever in order to prevent a bill from moving forward. Some have argued that this ability should be removed because it is too powerful and not democratic.

The House has a Speaker who is in charge of the House's calendar, which denotes which bills will be debated and when. The Senate does not have a similar position but is chaired by the Vice President, who casts the decisive vote in the event of a tie.

Both chambers are reliant on each other to pass laws. That is, both must approve a law for the law to be passed.

The Senate approves presidential nominations, such as Supreme Court justices, and the House has no say in the process. The Senate approves treaties with foreign countries. The House tends to be more concerned with taxes and spending. Impeachment hearings begin in the House and move to the Senate, which acts as a court.

The majority party in the House of Representatives has power to pass legislation much quicker. In the Senate, the majority still has the power to decide when a bill comes to the floor to be voted upon, but a single Senator can slow it down or stop it.

To become a law, a bill needs a simple majority vote of 51 out of 100 senators, but practically requires 60 votes to overcome a filibuster.

fil*i*bus*ter

> *the use of extreme dilatory tactics (as by making long speeches) in an attempt to delay or prevent action especially in a legislative assembly.*
>
> (Miriam-Webster)

How Does a Bill Become a Law?

All laws begin as ideas. Then, a Representative brings it to the table. A committee is assigned to study the bill. If the committee feels it has merits, the bill is put on a calendar so that the House of Representatives or the Senate can vote or debate on it. If it passes the scrutiny of the relevant chamber and the majority votes for it, the bill moves on to the second chamber.

The other chamber looks it over, proposes changes, votes on whether to pass the bill, and then releases it so that it can be amended or debated again.

After both Houses pass the bill, a conference committee looks at the versions produced by the House of Representatives and the Senate, examining differences and trying to reconcile them. The reconciled version of the bill returns to the House and Senate for a final vote.

The president then has ten days to sign the bill into law or veto it.

19. What are the two parts of the U.S. Congress?

- *Senate and House (of Representatives)*

See Question 18 for more information.

20. Name <u>one</u> power of the U.S. Congress. *

- *Writes laws*
- *Declares war*
- *Makes the federal budget*

21. How many U.S. Senators are there?

- *one hundred (100)*

Each of the fifty states is represented by two Senators. Before 1913, Senators were elected by state legislatures. Since 1913, Senators have been directly elected by the public.

When drafting the Constitution, smaller states threatened to leave and not be part of the new country of America, unless they had equal power to the larger states. Because the number of Representatives is equal for each state, states with small populations now have a large amount of influence at the federal level.

22. How long is a term for a U.S. senator?

- *six (6) years*

U.S. Senators are elected to serve for six years, and in any given year, only one-third of the Senate are up for reelection. Terms are staggered so that both seats from a state do not go up for election at the same time, unless a vacancy is being filled.

There is no limit to the number of terms a senator can serve.

23. Who is <u>one</u> of your state's U.S. Senators now?

- *Answers will vary.*

[District of Columbia residents and residents of U.S. territories should answer that D.C. (or the territory where the applicant lives) has no U.S. senators.]

24. How many voting members are in the House of Representatives?

- *four hundred thirty-five (435)*

The number of members is proportional to state population. Each state is guaranteed at least one member, and there is a maximum of 435 members for the nation. By law, the House currently has 435 voting members. Congress has maintained this size since the early 20th century, but it could change the number by statute.

25. How long is a term for a member of the House of Representatives?

- *two (2) years*

Members of the House of Representatives serve for two years and can be reelected every two years.

There is no limit to the number of terms a Congressmember can serve.

26. Why do U.S. representatives serve shorter terms than U.S. senators?

- *To more closely follow public opinion*

27. How many senators does each state have?

- *Two (2)*

28. Why does each state have two senators?

- *Equal representation (for small states)*
- *The Great Compromise (Connecticut Compromise)*

29. Name your U.S. Representative.

- *Answers will vary.*
  [Residents of territories with nonvoting Delegates or Resident Commissioners may provide the name of that Delegate or Commissioner. Also acceptable is any statement that the territory has no (voting) representatives in Congress.]

D.C. and the Territories

The District of Columbia and the five U.S. territories do not have voting members in the House or in the Senate. Each sends one non-voting member to the House. Washington, D.C., American Samoa, Guam, the Northern Mariana Islands, and the U.S. Virgin Islands each send a delegate. Puerto Rico sends a Resident Commissioner. These members can serve on committees and speak on the House floor, but they cannot vote on the final passage of legislation.

The population of each region is approximately:

- District of Columbia: 690,000
- Puerto Rico: 3,200,000
- American Samoa: 44,000
- Guam: 169,000
- Northern Mariana Islands: 56,000
- U.S. Virgin Islands: 87,000

That means that 4.2 million people currently do not have voting representation in Congress. Puerto Rico has a larger population than eighteen states, and D.C. has more people than either Vermont or Wyoming.

Puerto Rico, acquired by the U.S. in 1898, is the oldest colony in the modern world. The people cannot vote for President, nor do they receive the federal funding that states get. They have no Senators. A large number of Puerto Ricans have pursued statehood for the region, and efforts are ongoing. Puerto Rico's population would be eligible for four seats in the House, but with the total number capped at 435, seats would have to be taken away from other states.

30. What is the name of the Speaker of the House of Representatives now? *

- *Visit uscis.gov/citizenship/testupdates for the name of the Speaker of the House of Representatives.*

31. Who does a U.S. Senator represent?

- *Citizens of their state*
- *People of their state*

While members of the House of Representatives are elected to represent their district, Senators are elected to represent their entire state.

32. Who elects U.S. senators?

- *Citizens from their state*

Since the Seventeenth Amendment in 1913, voters in each state elect two senators. Senators serve six-year terms, with elections staggered so that about one-third of them are elected every two years.

33. Who does a member of the House of Representatives represent?

- *Citizens in their (congressional) district*
- *Citizens in their district*
- *People from their (congressional) district*
- *People in their district*

34. Who elects members of the House of Representatives?

- *Citizens from their (congressional) district*

35. Some states have more representatives than other states. Why?

- *(Because of) the state's population*
- *(Because) they have more people*
- *(Because) some states have more people*

The number of Representatives in the House is based on population. Some states, their population, and their number of Representatives are:

- California – 39,400,000 – 52
- Texas – 31,300,000 – 38
- Florida – 23,400,000 – 28
- New York – 19,900,000 – 26
- Washington – 8,000,000 – 10
- Hawaii – 1,400,000 – 2
- Wyoming – 600,000 - 1

36. The President of the United States is elected for how many years? *

- *Four (4) years*

The president of the United States of America is elected every four years, and the voting takes place on the first Tuesday after the first Monday in November of that year. Each presidential term is four years, and presidents are limited to two four-year terms.

Total service as president is capped at ten years. If a person enters office without election and remains for less than two years, they can then run for two full terms.

To run for president, you must be a natural-born U.S. citizen, at least thirty-five years old, and be a resident of the U.S. for at least fourteen years.

37. The President of the United States can serve only two terms. Why?

- *(Because of) the 22nd Amendment*
- *To keep the president from becoming too powerful*

38. What is the name of the President of the United States now?*

- *Visit uscis.gov/citizenship/testupdates for the name of the President of the United States.*

39. What is the name of the Vice President of the United States now?

- *Visit uscis.gov/citizenship/testupdates for the name of the Vice President of the United States.*

40. If the President can no longer serve, who becomes President?

- *The Vice President (of the United States)*

Line of Succession

If the president is unable to serve for some reason, the vice president will take over. If the vice president is not available, the Speaker of the House is next in line.

Accidental Presidents

There have been times when a sitting American president has died or resigned, and the vice president has had to take over. These people were not elected, and sometimes their own parties would not necessarily have chosen them to be president. Interestingly, only four of these people went on to win a presidential election in their own right.

JOHN TYLER (1790-1862)

"His Accidency" assumed office after William Henry Harrison (America's ninth president) died from pneumonia after just one month in the White House. John Tyler was the first president in American history to assume office due to their predecessor's death. He was from Virginia. Under his administration, Texas was offered statehood in 1845, and Tyler signed the bill for this just before leaving office. Tyler was a firm believer in the Constitution and wanted to faithfully adhere to its clauses.

MILLARD FILLMORE (1800-1874)

He was America's thirteenth president after his predecessor, Zachary Taylor, died. One of his significant accomplishments was that he staved off the Civil War for over ten years with the Compromise of 1850. Millard Fillmore also opened up trading between America and Japan through the Treaty of Kanagawa.

ANDREW JOHNSON (1865-1869)

He assumed office after President Abraham Lincoln was assassinated in 1865, right after the American Civil War ended. Johnson had to reconstruct the defeated South. Against him were radical Republicans in Congress, and Johnson was no match for them. The radicals passed laws to restrict the president, and Johnson ended up being impeached on eleven counts. He was tried by the Senate in 1868 and acquitted by one vote. Johnson was returned to the Senate in 1875, but died a few months later.

CHESTER ARTHUR (1881-1885)

He was the Twenty-First president of the United States and succeeded to the presidency after James A. Garfield was assassinated. Arthur was a wise statesman, firm and effective in administration, although he was unloved by his own party. Under his administration, he passed the first general federal immigration law. As a result, Chinese immigration was suspended for ten years and was later made permanent by Congress. He died in 1886.

THEODORE ROOSEVELT (1901-1909)

He became the youngest president in U.S. history at age forty-two, when he became president after the assassination of President McKinley. He emerged as a strong leader with progressive reforms and a robust foreign policy. 'Teddy' was the Twenty-Sixth president of the U.S. His face is depicted with those of Thomas Jefferson, George Washington, and Abraham Lincoln on Mount Rushmore.

His accomplishments included the construction of the Panama Canal and the establishment of foreign bases in the Caribbean. Roosevelt won the Nobel Peace Prize for mediating the Russo-Japanese war. He was the first accidental president to win a presidential election in his own right in 1904.

CALVIN COOLIDGE (1923-1929)

He was a politician and a lawyer who served as President Warren G. Harding's Vice President for about two and a half years. Harding died suddenly on August 2, 1923, and Coolidge became America's thirtieth president. He took a hard stand against administration scandals and abruptly dismissed the involved officials. The total federal debt shrank by one quarter during Coolidge's presidency, and he also signed the Immigration Act of 1924, which restricted immigration into the U.S. He was elected for a full four-year term in 1924.

HARRY S. TRUMAN (1945-1953)

He became president after the death of Franklin D. Roosevelt. After only eighty-two days as Vice President and "having met Roosevelt only twice", Harry S. Truman found himself president of the United States at the height of WWII. He was the president who made the crucial decision to order atomic bombs to be dropped on Hiroshima and Nagasaki, after which Japan surrendered.

Historians now rate Truman as one of the best presidents ever. Truman served two terms, and he implemented the Marshall Plan to rebuild the economy of Western Europe after the war. He also advanced African American civil rights. He died in 1972.

> *April 12th began as an ordinary day if such a thing could exist in America's capital city during the fourth full year of world war. In future, Harry Truman would remember this day as the day 'the whole weight of the moon and stars fell on me.'*
>
> —from *The Accidental President,* by Albert Baime, 2017.

LYNDON JOHNSON (1963-1969)

He was often referred to by his initials, L.B.J. He became president after the assassination of John F. Kennedy. He is renowned for passing a significant tax cut, the Clean Air Act, and the Civil Rights Act of 1964.

In 1964, Johnson won the presidency with an overwhelming 61% vote. He went on to create the two government-run health care programs, Medicare and Medicaid. During Johnson's presidency, three astronauts managed to reach the moon in 1968.

GERALD FORD (1974-1977)

He took office after the Watergate scandal, succeeding the first U.S. president ever to resign: Richard Nixon. After becoming president,

Ford announced an amnesty for those who had evaded the draft or deserted during the Vietnam War. In a controversial step, he also pardoned Richard Nixon on September 8, 1974.

41. Name <u>one</u> power of the president.

- *Signs bills into law*
- *Vetoes bills*
- *Enforces laws*
- *Commander in Chief (of the military)*
- *Chief diplomat*
- *Appoints federal judges*

42. Who is the Commander in Chief of the military?

- *The President (of the United States)*

In Article II, Section 2, Clause 1, the Constitution says,

> *The President shall be Commander in Chief of the Army and Navy of the United States, and of the Militia of the several States, when called into the actual Service of the United States; he may require the Opinion, in writing, of the principal Officer in each of the executive Departments, upon any Subject relating to the Duties of their respective Offices, and he shall have Power to grant Reprieves and Pardons for Offences against the United States, except in Cases of Impeachment.*

A legal advisor of the State Department once stated the following, which became widely circulated:

> *Under the Constitution, the President, in addition to being Chief Executive, is Commander in Chief of the*

Army and Navy. He holds the prime responsibility for the conduct of United States foreign relations. These duties carry very broad powers, including the power to deploy American forces abroad and commit them to military operations when the President deems such action necessary to maintain the security and defense of the United States.

In 1787 the world was a far larger place, and the framers probably had in mind attacks upon the United States. In the twentieth century, the world has grown much smaller. An attack on a country far from our shores can impinge directly on the Nation's security. In the SEATO treaty, for example, it is formally declared that an armed attack against Viet Nam would endanger the peace and security of the United States.

Under our Constitution it is the President who must decide when an armed attack has occurred. He has also the constitutional responsibility for determining what measures of defense are required when the peace and safety of the United States are endangered. If he considers that deployment of U.S. forces to South Viet Nam is required, and that military measures against the source of Communist aggression in North Viet Nam are necessary, he is constitutionally empowered to take those measures.

Some people oppose this position. They believe that the authority to start a war belongs entirely to Congress and that the president is only responsible for acting in cases of emergency.

43. Who signs bills to become laws?

- *The President (of the United States)*

When a bill is given to the president, they have 10 days, excluding

Sundays, to sign it and make it law. If the President does not sign during that time frame, the bill automatically becomes law unless Congress is not in session. If Congress is not in session at that time, the bill fails to become law.

44. Who vetoes bills? *

- *The President (of the United States)*

The Presentment Clause gives the president the power to veto bills passed along from Congress. Congress can override a veto, but it requires two-thirds vote of both Houses.

Examples of presidents and the number of times they have used the veto:

- George Washington - 2
- Thomas Jefferson – 0
- Grover Cleveland – 584
- Franklin D. Roosevelt – 635
- Ronald Reagan – 78
- Bill Clinton - 37
- Barack Obama – 12
- Joseph Biden – 13

45. Who appoints federal judges?

- *The President (of the United States)*

46. The executive branch has many parts. Name one.

- *President (of the United States)*
- *Cabinet*
- *Federal departments and agencies*

47. What does the President's Cabinet do?

- *Advises the President (of the United States)*

The Cabinet is a group of people who advise the president. They generally meet with the president in the room next to the Oval Office in the West Wing of the White House.

The Cabinet is made up of the heads of departments who were appointed by the president. These people have full control over their departments but they have no executive powers like the president.

There are twenty-five members:

- Vice President
- fifteen department heads
- ten Cabinet-level officials

The Senate confirms appointees, but the President can dismiss people from the Cabinet at any time without approval. This does not include the vice president.

In order of succession, the department heads include the following:

- Vice President
- Department of State
- Department of the Treasury
- Department of Defense
- Department of Justice
- Department of the Interior
- Department of Agriculture
- Department of Commerce
- Department of Labor
- Department of Health and Human Services
- Department of Housing and Urban Development
- Department of Transportation
- Department of Energy

- Department of Education
- Department of Veteran Affairs
- Department of Homeland Security

Cabinet-level officials include the following:

- White House Chief of Staff
- Environmental Protection Agency
- Office of Management & Budget
- U.S. Trade Representative
- U.S. Mission to the United Nations
- Council of Economic Advisors
- Small Business Administration

48. What are two Cabinet-level positions?

- *Attorney General*
- *Secretary of Agriculture*
- *Secretary of Commerce*
- *Secretary of Education*
- *Secretary of Energy*
- *Secretary of Health and Human Services*
- *Secretary of Homeland Security*
- *Secretary of Housing and Urban Development*
- *Secretary of the Interior*
- *Secretary of Labor*
- *Secretary of State*
- *Secretary of Transportation*
- *Secretary of the Treasury*
- *Secretary of Veterans Affairs*

- *Secretary of War*
- *Vice President*
- *Administrator of the Environmental Protection Agency*
- *Administrator of the Small Business Administration*
- *Director of the Central Intelligence Agency*
- *Director of the Office of Management and Budget*
- *Director of National Intelligence*
- *United States Trade Representative*

How Much Do They Make?

As of January 2023, most heads of departments and the vice president earn about $235,000 per year.

In contrast, the president earns about $400,000, and justices of the Supreme Court earn about $300,000.

49. Why is the Electoral College important?

- *It decides who is elected president*
- *It provides a compromise between the popular election of the president and congressional selection*

50. What is one part of the judicial branch?

- *Supreme Court*
- *Federal Courts*

51. What does the judicial branch do?

- *Reviews laws*
- *Explains laws*
- *Resolves disputes (disagreements)*
- *Decides if a law goes against the Constitution*

While the legislative branch of government makes laws, the judicial branch adjudicates them. If someone believes that a law is wrong, they can file a suit, and the courts will review the law to see if it goes against the Constitution, the highest law of the land. If there is uncertainty regarding how a law is applied, they will decide the meaning of the law and how to apply the law in real situations.

52. What is the highest court in the United States? *

- *Supreme Court*

Figure 6: © Shutterstock / Jon Bilous, used under license

The Supreme Court is the highest court in the U.S. If cases in lower courts are appealed, the Supreme Court has the final say. The Supreme Court has jurisdiction over cases affecting ambassadors, public ministers and consuls, and when a state is a party. The court can strike down presidential directives if they violate the Constitution or the law.

In the Constitution, Article II, Section 2, Clause 2 gives the president the power to nominate the justices of the Supreme Court. They are then confirmed by the Senate.

53. How many seats are on the Supreme Court?

- *Nine (9)*

55. How long do Supreme Court justices serve?

- *(For) life*
- *Lifetime appointment*
- *(Until) retirement*

The Supreme Court is made up of nine judges with one Chief Justice and eight Associate Justices. They are appointed for life, unless they retire, resign, or are impeached and removed.

- *Visit uscis.gov/citizenship/testupdates for the number of justices on the Supreme Court.*

56. Supreme Court justices serve for life. Why?

- *To be independent (of politics)*
- *To limit outside (political) influence*

57. Who is the Chief Justice of the United States now?

- *Visit uscis.gov/citizenship/testupdates for the name of the Chief Justice of the United States.*

58. Name one power that is only for the federal government.

- *Print paper money*
- *Mint coins*
- *Declare war*
- *Create an army*
- *Make treaties*
- *Set foreign policy*

The powers of the federal government are expressly listed in the Constitution and include the following:

- To create and collect taxes, duties, imposts, and excises to pay for the general welfare of the U.S.
- To borrow money for the U.S.
- To regulate commerce between nations, states, and American tribes.
- To make a uniform rule of naturalization and laws on bankruptcy.
- To make money, regulate its value, and punish counterfeiting.
- To regulate weights and measures.
- To secure intellectual property.
- To establish post offices.
- To promote arts and sciences.
- To establish courts inferior to the Supreme Court.
- To define and punish piracy.
- To declare war, grant letters of marque, and to make rules about capturing land and water.
- To create, govern, regulate, and support armies.
- To create, govern, regulate, and support a navy.

- To organize, arm, and discipline a militia.
- To make laws.
- To punish treason.
- To create treaties and foreign agreements

There are also implied powers for the federal government, including the following.

- Creating a national bank
- Setting the minimum wage
- Creating labor laws
- Regulating immigration
- Creating a military draft

59. Name one power that is only for the states.

- *Provide schooling and education*
- *Provide protection (police)*
- *Provide safety (fire departments)*
- *Give a driver's license*
- *Approve zoning and land use*

Under the Tenth Amendment, states have powers over everything that is not granted to the federal government. This usually includes health care, education, emergency services (police, fire departments), roads and driver's licenses, and zoning and land use.

60. What is the purpose of the 10th Amendment?

- *(It states that the) powers not given to the federal government belong to the states or to the people.*

61. Who is the Governor of your state now? *

- *Answers will vary.*

[District of Columbia residents should answer that D.C. does not have a governor.]

62. What is the capital of your state?*

- *Answers will vary.*

[District of Columbia residents should answer that D.C. is not a state and does not have a capital. Residents of U.S. territories should name the capital of the territory.]

★ ★ ★ ★ ★

QUESTIONS 63-89: RIGHTS AND RESPONSIBILITIES

63. There are four amendments to the U.S. Constitution about who can vote. Describe one of them.

- *Citizens eighteen (18) and older (can vote)*
- *You don't have to pay (a poll tax) to vote*
- *Any citizen can vote. (Women and men can vote)*
- *A male citizen of any race (can vote)*

Amendments

In 1870, the Fifteenth Amendment gave African American men the right to vote. Unfortunately, not all were able to vote. Some states made it more difficult to vote by requiring literacy tests and other barriers, such as poll taxes that charged people to vote.

In 1920, the Nineteenth Amendment gave women the right to vote.

In 1964, the Twenty-Fourth Amendment eliminated poll taxes. That allowed anyone to vote regardless of their economic situation. Even those who are homeless can vote.

In 1971, the Twenty-Sixth Amendment lowered the voting age from twenty-one to eighteen. The desire to change partly came from the fact that men could join the armed forces at the age of eighteen. It seemed strange to many people that you could sign up to fight and die for your country but you had no voice in how the country was run. Proponents used the slogan, "Old enough to fight, old enough to vote."

64. Who can vote in federal elections, run for federal office, and serve on a jury in the United States?

- *Citizens*
- *Citizens of the United States*
- *U.S. citizens*

Who Can Vote?

Almost all U.S. citizens can vote. This includes those living overseas, those born abroad and who have never lived in the U.S., and dual citizens living in the U.S. or outside of it. You must meet your state's requirements, but you can still meet those even if you are homeless.

You must be eighteen years old on or before election day. Most states will allow you to register in advance if you will be eighteen on election day.

Figure 6: © Shutterstock / Frame Stock Footage, used under license

Who Cannot Vote?

Those who cannot vote include noncitizens, including permanent residents. Depending on the state, some people convicted of certain felonies cannot vote while serving time, and some people with a mental disability may not be able to vote.

U.S. citizens living in U.S. territories cannot vote for president.

65. What are three rights of everyone living in the United States?

- *Freedom of expression*
- *Freedom of speech*
- *Freedom of assembly*
- *Freedom to petition the government*
- *Freedom of religion*
- *The right to bear arms*

Freedoms of Expression, Speech, and Assembly

Throughout history and around the world, there have been many tyrannical governments. These come to be when abusers of power take more and more money and power for themselves at the expense of others. Taking power becomes easier when they keep people ignorant and silent.

In order for democracy to really work, voters need the freedom to become informed about issues. That means being able to hear all perspectives on each issue and hearing all the facts so that they can make their own judgements without government limits or interference.

The freedom of assembly allows people to gather to hear the things being said. The freedoms of expression and speech allow people to speak, publish, read, and view information freely without fear of reprisal or censorship. This makes it very difficult for people to hide the truth, to bury corruption, and to get away with bad actions.

The First Amendment applies only to the government. It does not prevent individuals and businesses from restricting speech. For example, social media companies can restrict and regulate speech on their platforms.

Freedom to Petition the Government

If citizens are not allowed to challenge the government and demand change, their opinions and needs will not matter, and rulers will do whatever they want. When they do bad things that hurt citizens, if the people can not speak up about it, leaders will not face consequences for their actions. This encourages them to repeat those bad actions. The freedom to petition the government allows people to challenge how leaders operate. It allows people to challenge corruption and evil.

Originally, this freedom was added to the Constitution to allow citizens to confront government in order to redress their grievances. Today, the meaning has expanded to give citizens the right to demand that government use its power to further the interest and prosperity of the people. It is about more than speaking up when the government does bad things. It is about demanding the government act in the people's best interest at all times.

Citizens can petition all branches of the government.

FIRST SIGNIFICANT USE

The freedom to petition the government was first really used to advocate for the end to slavery. People sent thousands of petitions to Congress, but members of the House of Representatives who supported slavery got the House to issue gag rules to silence people and stop them from discussing the issue. The Senate did something similar. Some members of the House and the Senate were proud slave owners. They and their friends owned plantations and businesses that relied on slavery, and they wanted to protect their interests.

President John Quincy Adams and others managed to get these rules repealed several years later on the basis that they were unconstitutional.

Freedom of Religion

When a nation has an official religion, there is often a lot of pressure to conform to official practices and official beliefs. There can also be a lot of discrimination and hostility toward anyone who does not conform exactly to these practices and beliefs. In Europe, this has caused a lot of people pain and suffering. Wars have been fought because of it.

Therefore, when the founders of the U.S. were creating their new nation, they wanted to create a place where everyone could safely choose what to believe and how to worship, or not to worship. They wanted a land free of discrimination and persecution.

The United States is made up of people from many parts of the world with a wide range of spiritual beliefs. The principle of separation of church and state means the government cannot favor or discriminate against anyone based on their religion or spiritual practices. This protects each person's right to live according to their own beliefs.

The Right to Bear Arms

The United States was founded during a time when armies were smaller and regular citizens could mobilize to become an effective, if untrained, military force. This was especially true during the American Revolution. When the armies of Britain tried to stop the thirteen colonies from standing up for themselves, it was the militia that won American freedom. However, there was no guarantee that Britain would not come back or that some other country would not want to take the colonies for themselves.

When writing the Constitution, some founders wanted the people to be able to protect themselves. They wrote the Second Amendment to give the people the right to possess and carry weapons in case of confrontation.

HISTORY OF THE RIGHT TO BEAR ARMS

Throughout history, English kings and other tyrants were able to suppress their subjects by taking away their weapons so that only the ruler's people were armed. Then, no matter what the leader did, the people could not fight back.

In England in 1689, the right to bear arms was added to the English Bill of Rights, one hundred years before the same was done in America.

CONTROVERSY

Despite being a socially and economically advanced country and thriving democracy, the U.S. suffers from far more gun violence than all other high-income countries. This is partly because so many weapons are in private possession.

In other countries, laws regulating and eliminating gun ownership have been extremely successful at reducing gun violence. In the U.S., many attempts have been made to make it more difficult to obtain and own firearms. Many laws have been proposed to limit the kinds of firearms people can have because those weapons have become increasingly powerful over time. These attempts to reduce gun ownership in order to curb gun violence have largely failed because the minority who support gun rights have been very vocal and well-funded when they have lobbied the government.

The majority of gun violence comes from suicides, but homicides are still very significant. Many mass shootings shootings take place, even in schools. The leading cause of death for U.S. children aged sixteen through nineteen is gun violence.

PRESIDENTIAL ASSASSINATIONS

Eleven assassination attempts have been made against U.S. presidents using guns. Four presidents were killed.

- Abraham Lincoln survived one attack but was later shot and killed in a second attack.

- James A. Garfield was shot twice and later died of complications from his wounds.
- William McKinley was shot twice and fatally wounded, later dying of infection.
- John F. Kennedy was killed in 1963.
- Andrew Jackson, Harry S. Truman, and Gerald Ford (twice) were shot at but survived unharmed.
- Ronald Reagan was shot and wounded and is the only U.S. president to survive an assassination attempt while in office.
- Theodore Roosevelt was shot and wounded during his presidential campaign during a speech, refusing to go to a hospital until he had finished speaking.
- Franklin Delano Roosevelt was shot at while president-elect, surviving unharmed, though the Chicago mayor with him at the time was killed and others injured.

These events led to the National Firearms Act of 1934 and the Gun Control Act of 1968.

66. What do we show loyalty to when we say the Pledge of Allegiance? *

- *The United States*
- *The flag*

The Pledge of Allegiance

> *"I pledge allegiance to the Flag of the United States of America, and to the Republic for which it stands, one Nation under God, indivisible, with liberty and justice for all."*

The pledge is a promise of loyalty to the United States and American values.

Composed in 1892 by author Francis Bellamy, the Pledge of Allegiance was initially used as a military salute. After reciting the words to the flag, soldiers had to extend one arm toward it. Later, people felt that it mimicked the Nazi salute too much, and the extension of the arm was omitted at formal gatherings. It later became the practice to hold your hand over your heart instead.

The Pledge of Allegiance is taught and recited in schools, Congressional sessions, government meetings, citizenship ceremonies, etc. Accepted by Congress in 1942, the pledger promises to defend the U.S. Constitution, obey the laws of the United States, and be loyal to America.

67. Name two promises that new citizens make in the Oath of Allegiance.

- *Give up loyalty to other countries*
- *Defend the (U.S.) Constitution*
- *Obey the laws of the United States*
- *Serve in the military (if needed)*
- *Serve (help, do important work for) the nation (if needed)*
- *Be loyal to the United States*

Oath of Allegiance

After passing the civics test, all future citizens are expected to swear an oath of allegiance to the republic and the flag, honoring the American nation.

> *I hereby declare, on oath, that I absolutely and entirely renounce and abjure all allegiance and fidelity to any*

foreign prince, potentate, state, or sovereignty of whom or which I have heretofore been a subject or citizen; that I will support and defend the Constitution and laws of the United States of America against all enemies, foreign and domestic; that I will bear true faith and allegiance to the same; that I will bear arms on behalf of the United States when required by the law; that I will perform noncombatant service in the Armed Forces of the United States when required by the law; that I will perform work of national importance under civilian direction when required by the law; and that I take this obligation freely without any mental reservation or purpose of evasion; so help me God.

The phrase "so help me God" is optional.

If a prospective citizen is unable or unwilling to promise to fight in the military due to "religious training or belief," they may request not to include that part of the oath.

Why the Oath?

The Oath of Allegiance is a promise. That promise is part of building trust. Becoming a citizen is a social contract between the immigrant and established citizens. The people already living in America are extending faith and trust in the new arrival, and the promise made by the new immigrant is that they will be a good member of their new community.

68. How can people become United States citizens?

- *Be born in the United States, under the conditions set by the 14th Amendment*
- *Naturalize*

- *Derive citizenship (under conditions set by Congress)*

69. What are two examples of civic participation in the United States?

- *Vote*
- *Run for office*
- *Join a political party*
- *Help with a campaign*
- *Join a civic group*
- *Join a community group*
- *Give an elected official your opinion (on an issue)*
- *Contact elected officials*
- *Support or oppose an issue or policy*
- *Write to a newspaper*

Citizen Participation in U.S. Democracy

To participate in the democracy of the United States, you must be a U.S. citizen. A citizen is anyone born in the U.S., anyone with U.S. citizen parents, or anyone who applies and is accepted as a citizen. Citizens can engage in the following democratic activities to help maintain and improve their new country.

VOTE

If you are a citizen and over eighteen years of age, you can vote and start participating in the democracy. Voting is one of the most fundamental things you can do to engage as a citizen in your democracy.

JOIN A POLITICAL PARTY OR RUN FOR OFFICE

Those in public office are not the only members of political parties. Each party has millions of dedicated members who support the party's objectives by building public support, debating policy, building up new leaders, and raising funds.

If you have the right passion and skills, you can also run for office yourself, becoming a champion of your community. There are offices at the municipal, state, and federal level.

HELP WITH A CAMPAIGN

There are plenty of ways you can help with a campaign, including:

- becoming a community champion for various policies and those running for office.
- building connections in both political and civic fields.
- organizing events.
- fundraising.
- canvassing: knocking on doors to gain support and votes
- social media activity.
- registering voters.

JOIN A CIVIC OR COMMUNITY GROUP

There are many nonprofit corporations, associations, and political entities, as well as official government organizations. Examples include parent-teacher and neighborhood watch associations, as well as charities like the Salvation Army, Feeding America, United Way, and Habitat for Humanity.

GIVE AN ELECTED OFFICIAL YOUR OPINION, CALL SENATORS AND REPRESENTATIVES

People elected to office are expected to represent the views of those who voted for them. You can voice your views to lawmakers and ask them to consider voting in ways that reflect those views. This keeps them informed so they can better do their jobs.

You can voice your opinions directly as well as publicly, such as writing to the news media or interacting with others on social media.

70. What is one way Americans can serve their country?

- *Vote*
- *Pay taxes*
- *Obey the law*
- *Serve in the military*
- *Run for office*
- *Work for local, state, or federal government*

71. Why is it important to pay federal taxes?

- *Required by law*
- *All people pay to fund the federal government*
- *Required by the (U.S.) Constitution (16th Amendment)*
- *Civic duty*

Internal Revenue Service (IRS)

You can find the tax deadline and everything else you need to know about filing your taxes on the official IRS website: https://www.irs.gov/.

72. It is important for all men age eighteen through twenty-five to register for the Selective Service. Name one reason why.

- *Required by law*
- *Civic duty*
- *Makes the draft fair, if needed*

What is Selective Service?

The Selective Service began in 1917, when the U.S. was at war with Germany during World War I.

The Selective Service maintains a database of male U.S. citizens and other U.S. residents who are potentially subject to military conscription (the draft). That means that if the U.S. goes to war and runs out of regular soldiers, they may call up citizens to serve, as well. They do this using a public lottery system.

You must register within thirty days of your eighteenth birthday. All male U.S. citizens and immigrant noncitizens between the ages eighteen and twenty-five are required by law to register.

★ ★ ★ ★ ★

QUESTIONS 73-89: COLONIAL PERIOD AND INDEPENDENCE

73. The colonists came to America for many reasons. Name one.

- *Freedom*
- *Political liberty*
- *Religious freedom*
- *Economic opportunity*
- *Escape persecution*

Why Europeans Migrated to the Americas

Europe has a very long history of human civilization. By the fifteenth century, there were multiple established nations in close competition. However, none were able to grow as much as they wanted to because other countries kept them in check. Many European countries encouraged exploration, seeking new territory and wealth.

When the Americas were discovered, England, France, and other countries were eager to send their people overseas and develop colonies. There are five important reasons that drove people overseas.

FREEDOM AND POLITICAL LIBERTY

European countries were primarily ruled by monarchs with absolute power and dominated by the nobility, a wealthy class with incredible power and position that was handed down in families from one generation to the next. For most people, the social system they lived in kept them down. They could never acquire significant wealth. They could not rise to positions of influence or power. Royalty and nobility locked them out of such things.

Many people were desperate for freedom. They wished to live in a society that allowed everyone to participate more equally. They wanted the common people to have a voice in government. The discovery of new lands far away from those in power could give people a chance to escape the oppression under which they had been living. It gave them hope that they could develop something new.

Freedom and political liberty became part of the foundation of American government and society. Those values led to America becoming a devoutly democratic country, and they are also why America encourages other countries around the world to embrace democracy.

RELIGIOUS FREEDOM

While most Europeans were members of Christian faiths, Christianity was divided into multiple factions, most of which were not just in competition with each other, but openly hostile to one another. Going to a new land meant being free from the power of established churches. In the American colonies, people would be free to develop their own religious factions and worship as they wished without being punished for it.

ECONOMIC OPPORTUNITY

At the time the Americas were discovered by Europeans, most people in Europe were poor. Society was primarily agricultural, and most people were farmers. Wealth and power were tightly controlled by a small group of social elite, the nobility. They absolutely did not want to share any money or power with the common people. But even for the nobility the situation was strained. Wealth and titles were usually passed from father to oldest son. If the family had multiple sons, the younger sons often struggled to find positions for themselves.

When the Americas were discovered, creating overseas colonies made way for new economic opportunities. Colonists could build new farms that were much bigger than those in Europe, and the farms would be owned by the farmers, not the nobility. New colonies needed new businesses, and a need for transoceanic shipping arose. The new lands allowed people to take control of their lives like never before, and to keep more of the wealth they worked so hard to create. It was a place where economic freedom was possible.

ESCAPE PERSECUTION

In Europe, many groups of people faced discrimination. This could have been due to their religion, where their ancestors lived, the color of their skin, or almost any other reason. Tired of being hated for who or what they were, some people saw the New World as a chance to escape the hatred and unfairness with which they lived. They felt they could create a new society where everyone was treated equally, no matter their differences. This desire became a very important part of American culture, and is a value upheld today more than ever. It was also an important consideration when creating a new government in

America. The Founding Fathers wanted a society where people were no longer persecuted.

The First Colonies

In 1607, the British established the first permanent colony in North America (via the London Company) at Jamestown on Chesapeake Bay. Some 104 English men and boys established the settlement. Captain John Smith, of Jamestown, explored the nearby coast in 1614 and named the region New England because he thought the climate and soil were just like those of his mother country.

Over the next decade, some 1,700 settlers made their way to the colony. Life was difficult for the colonists. They faced harsh winters and had a lot of difficulty growing food. By 1617, only 351 settlers were left out of the originals who had come. Then, because of frequent wars with local Native Americans, the London Company went bankrupt, and the British Crown took over the Colony of Virginia.

Figure 7: © Shutterstock / Everett Collection Footage, used under license

Other colonies followed: the Town of Saint George in Bermuda; Plymouth Colony, with settlers who arrived on the *Mayflower*; and the Newfoundland Colony. The colonists farmed tobacco, traded fur and other materials, and fished. A lot of their production was shipped back home to England.

Early colonists struggled. The residents of Plymouth, for example, were not adequately prepared for their new environment. They only survived the first winter in the New World thanks to the Pokanokets, a Native American tribe that controlled the area. The Pokanokets had suffered terribly due to a viral epidemic lasting from 1616 to 1618.

To protect themselves against other tribes, they allied themselves with the newcomers from Europe. During the colony's first few years, these Native Americans supplied the colonists with essential foodstuffs.

In time, the Europeans became well-established. They brought firearms, cattle, pigs, and horses to the continent.

The English marveled at the trees they found in America. Growing straight and tall, many of the trees grew up to ten meters (almost thirty-three feet) tall. In the 1620s and 1630s, soon after staking their claims to the new territories in Plymouth and beyond, colonists started felling the forests. They built houses, churches, and ships to sustain their way of life. Shipbuilding became one of the region's first major industries and remained one of the most important industries for a long time. They also had to fence in their croplands to prevent them from being overrun by cattle, sheep, and hogs.

More colonies were formed, and they later became the original thirteen American states. By 1700, about 250,000 English colonists called America their home.

74. Who lived in America before the Europeans arrived? *

- *American Indians*
- *Native Americans*

Native American Tribes in the U.S. Today

A general result of the frontier process was that Native Americans were displaced as the colonists moved in. Native Americans became confined to smaller tracts of land or were forced to migrate or disperse. Settlers took the land and considered themselves sovereign owners of it. However, tribal groups survived, and today many Native American tribes are still present in the U.S.

Federally Recognized Native American Tribes

In 1974, an unrecognized Native American tribe brought a land claim to court. In another court case, tribes demanded that the U.S. government recognize Aboriginal titles. Cases like these eventually led to the Indian Self-Determination and Educational Assistant Act of 1975, which legitimized tribal entities.

Recognized is a legal term. It means that the United States acknowledges a Native American tribe as an existing sovereign entity that can govern itself and is entitled to certain federal benefits, protections, and services. This recognition is based on a government-to-government relationship established through laws and treaties. While some tribes have adopted the U.S. Constitution, others operate under their own systems of governance.

The main criteria for being a federally recognized tribe is that there must be a government-to-government relationship with the United States. The designation comes with powers, obligations, responsibilities, and limitations. Recognized tribes get funding and services from the Bureau of Indian Affairs.

U.S. states have no authority over tribal governments, unless authorized to do so by Congress. However, tribal entities can choose to work together with their state governments, and they frequently do so by collaborating and cooperating on environmental and law enforcement issues.

At present, there are 574 federally recognized tribes in the U.S. including: the Cherokee, Navajo, Sioux, Chippewa, Inuit, and the Choctaw.

Terminology

The first humans to establish themselves in the Americas are known by a variety of terms, such as Indigenous peoples, First Nations peoples, Natives, Indians, Native Americans, and American Indians. Some terms remain in use while others have fallen out of use and some have become unacceptable. Terminology can be an important and sensitive subject for many people.

Indigenous comes from Latin and means "sprung from the land, native." It is a broad term without a clear definition, and different people have either provided their own definition or refused to define it. In North America, the term refers to First Nations, Inuit, and Métis peoples (people with Indigenous and European mixed ancestry).

Native Americans or American Indians refers to the organized tribal societies that were present when Europeans first colonized the U.S. These societies had government structures, traded, went to war, and used diplomacy. The names of these tribes are the answers to Question 87.

The term Indian came from a misunderstanding. Early explorer, Christopher Columbus, was looking to find a way to sail from Europe to India, in Asia. Going around Africa took a long time. Believing the world to be round, he sailed west. Europeans did not know of the Americas at that time, so when they first landed and met the local peoples, they referred to them as Indians, people of India. This term is considered by some to be outdated and even offensive. However, it is still used in legal and official definitions that were created many years ago.

The terms Native and Aboriginal have also been used for many years and appear in some legal and official usage. However, they have also fallen out of favor because some suggest that the former is too vague and the latter carries negative connotations.

75. What group of people was taken and sold as slaves?

- *Africans*
- *People from Africa*

Slavery in America

Many colonies had farms and plantations with crops that required a lot of labor to grow, such as sugar and cotton. The size of a farm was also limited to what the owner and their family could work by themselves. Families often found it difficult to survive on their farm because they were forced to sell all of their goods to England only, and England forced prices down. They unfairly paid farmers in the colonies less in order to create larger profits in England. This kept colonists poor and dependent on England while rich people in England got even richer.

Some colonists wanted more laborers just to survive. Other colonists dreamed of becoming rich and wanted to build bigger and bigger farms. Some of those settlers utilized slavery to increase their production. Most slaves came from Africa. Indigenous people were also enslaved, but on a much smaller scale.

By the middle of the sixteenth century, roughly four hundred people of African descent, most of them slaves, lived around Boston and other Atlantic ports. The number of slaves increased until there were about two slaves for every one hundred New Englanders during most of the colonial era.

The business of obtaining slaves in Africa and shipping them to Europe and the Americas for sale was called the Atlantic Slave Trade. More than 12 million slaves were eventually shipped out of West Africa between 1526 and 1867, first sold to Europe, and eventually in America starting in the 1600s. A lot of people came from the Bight of Biafra (modern day Nigeria) and Angola. After the late 1800s, the volume increased. The decade 1821 through 1830 saw 80,000 people per year crossing the Atlantic on slave ships. By 1825, about 25% of the U.S. population was of African descent.

For slaves, the transatlantic voyage was a nightmare due to disease, suicide, and sometimes uprisings. Slave ships were breeding grounds for yellow fever, malaria, scurvy, dysentery, measles, and other illnesses. Almost 20% of all slaves died during transit.

The Royal African Company gained a monopoly on the English slave trade starting in 1672. The company became the largest single business in the Atlantic Slave Trade and maintained seventeen forts to run their business. Some of its agents made fortunes. By the time the company's monopoly expired in 1712, individual illegal traders had also entered the market. By the early eighteenth century, these independent traders carried most of the African slaves to America.

Certain coastal rulers in Africa served as intermediaries, allowing slave trade forts (that were effectively prisons) on their land. They happily captured and sold their fellow Africans, filling European ships with people as trade goods. These rulers were able to gain great wealth and obtain rare goods, such as foreign textiles, alcohol, tobacco, and guns, which made them even more powerful.

Although the American Congress outlawed the African slave trade in 1808, the domestic slave trade continued until well into the 1860s.

76. What war did the Americans fight to win independence from Britain?

- *American Revolution*
- *The (American) Revolutionary War*
- *War for (American) Independence*

77. Name one reason why the Americans declared independence from Britain.

- *High taxes*
- *Taxation without representation*
- *British soldiers stayed in Americans' houses (boarding, quartering)*
- *They did not have self-government*
- *Boston Massacre*
- *Boston Tea Party (Tea Act)*
- *Stamp Act*
- *Sugar Act*
- *Townshend Acts*
- *Intolerable (Coercive) Acts*

Why America Declared Independence

Initially, American colonists were under the rule of the British Crown, but the Crown largely left the immigrants to their own devices. While the Spanish and Portuguese found immediate profits mining gold and silver in the Americas, British colonies were largely agricultural to begin with, and small, so the government focused more on simply grabbing as much land as possible rather than making money from it.

However, this changed in 1765, when Britain realized that the colonies had finally matured and it was sitting on a tax goldmine. After establishing so many colonies and fighting several wars, the British Empire was deeply in debt. It had the ideal solution for new revenue: to tax colonists in the Americas.

In 1764, Britain passed the Sugar Act, also known as the American Revenue Act and the American Duties Act. An earlier tax had been imposed in 1733 on molasses but had never been effectively collected because colonists had been able to get away with not paying. The Sugar Act was meant to change that. It imposed a lower tax rate, but increased enforcement. This signaled to the colonies that Britain's previously relaxed attitude to the colonies was changing, and that it would become more serious about collecting revenue from the colonies in the future.

In 1765, Britain passed the Stamp Act. Britain created a colonial tax, saying that all printed materials in the colonies had to be made with officially stamped paper from London. This included legal documents, newspapers and magazines, playing cards, and anything else that used printed paper. Stamped paper could only be purchased with British currency, not colonial currency, making it extra expensive. The tax was very unpopular. While Britain reasoned that the tax was needed to pay for the French and Indian War, the colonists objected, saying they would had nothing to do with the war and should not have to pay for it.

In 1767, Britain passed the Townshend Acts. They created a tax on goods going from Britain to the colonies, such as dishware, glass, lead, and more. Benjamin Franklin had previously told Britain's

Parliament that they intended to manufacture their own goods rather than pay high prices and duties on British goods. The Americans wanted to become more self-reliant and lower their expenses. The Townshend Acts imposed duties on goods that would be difficult for the Americans to make, especially on tea.

The money raised by the Townshend Acts would also be partially used to pay for British officials in the colonies, such as governors and judges. This would encourage them to be more loyal to Britain rather than the colony.

After already struggling for decades, the colonists, who were finally beginning to enjoy the fruits of their labor, deeply resented these selfish changes and increasing tax burdens. In 1770, they began to protest. Americans first responded by boycotting British goods. Britain answered by sending troops to quell the protest.

Americans first responded to these troops with snowball-throwing and name-calling. Then the British fired shots at an angry mob. Five colonists were killed and others wounded, inciting further rage towards Britain. This fight is known as the Boston Massacre.

Following the massacre, the Townshend Acts were ended in 1770, except for the tax on tea. Protests against the high tax on tea led to an event called the Boston Tea Party in 1773.

Colonists, disguised as American Indians, defiantly dumped 342 chests of very valuable tea into the harbor at Griffin's Wharf in Boston. The tea belonged to the British East India Company, a huge and extremely powerful company that controlled trade. Ruining the tea was extremely costly for them, and it robbed the government of taxes. According to one eyewitness, the chests of tea "piled up in the low tide as haystacks." It was the colonists' first major act of defiance against British rule.

When left alone during the early decades, settlers enjoyed their freedom and independence. Britain provided very little aid, but also did not tax them, nor were they around to enforce arbitrary laws. However, heavy new taxes placed an unfair burden on the colonists. Taxes are paid to governments to fund public services, such as water and sanitation, fire and police, education, and health care. The colonists felt that they did not have any form of representation in the British government, and the government provided no services in the colonies. Therefore, it was wrong for the colonies to be taxed.

They also resented that British soldiers were free to use civilian houses without providing the owners compensation. Britain had often been at war with other European nations and Indigenous tribes. Sometimes, that meant sending soldiers to the colonies, where soldiers were quartered in civilian houses. They could barge into someone's house whenever they wanted, sleeping in their beds and eating their food, disrupting people's lives, scaring families, and causing expenses. Colonists often felt violated by this personal intrusion, and more so when they were not compensated for it.

In 1774, to punish the colonies for defying Britain's rule, Britain passed the Intolerable Acts, also known as the Coercive of Insufferable Acts. There were four acts. The Boston Port Act closed the port of Boston until the colonists paid for the tea they had destroyed and accepted British rule. The Massachusetts Government Act took away the colonies' charter of government and placed them directly under British rule, removing any voice colonists had in their own governing. The Administration of Justice Act allowed the governor to move trials to Britain if they believed a fair trial could not be had in the colony. Witnesses in a trial would have to travel all the way to Britain at their own expense. The Quartering Act said that soldiers would now be quartered in empty buildings instead of colonists' houses.

Finally, the colonists had had enough. The colonists wanted their own government. They wanted to decide their own laws and escape British tyranny. However, requests for self-government were absolutely denied. Britain did not want to give up territorial control; did not want to lose tax and trade revenue; and did not want to look weak by giving into colonial demands.

This led to the American Revolution and America's declaration of independence from England on July 4, 1776.

The Battle of Bunker Hill

This was the first major battle of the American Revolution. Two months earlier, the British tried to seize American military stores and suppress the colonists, leading to battles at Lexington and Concord. The colonists then organized themselves in defense and began the Siege of Boston, leading to the Battle of Bunker Hill on June 17, 1775.

Fifteen thousand colonial troops gathered to confront the British. At first, they held the British off, but the colonists eventually had to flee when they ran out of ammunition.

Although the British defeated the Americans there, the colonists proved that they could hold their own against the British. The British also lost twice as many soldiers as the Americans. This gave the Americans the belief that they could win.

Washington Crossing the Delaware (The Battle of Trenton)

On December 25 and 26 of 1776, George Washington and the Continental Army began a series of secret maneuvers that led to the attack of the British garrison at Trenton. Trenton was filled with German mercenaries who had been hired by the British. Crossing the icy Delaware River to reach their target is considered one of the most logistically challenging operations of the war.

After winning the attack on the garrison, Washington took prisoners and supplies and then retreated back over the river. They then crossed the river a third time to attack and defeat British reinforcements twice. The battle bolstered American morale.

The Battles of Saratoga

The Battles of Saratoga happened between September and October 1777. The British sent an army south from Canada, hoping to join other British armies from Lake Ontario and New York. These two armies never arrived.

The Americans surrounded the force coming from Canada. The British won the first battle despite being outnumbered but were defeated in the second when the Americans were supplied with reinforcements. The British were outnumbered three to one and were forced to surrender.

Before the battle, the British had regarded the colonies with contempt, thinking that they would never be able to stand up to the formidable British Army. The loss at Saratoga taught them that the Americans could not be underestimated.

The American victory also encouraged France to throw its support behind the Americans, forming the Franco-American alliance, which drew the French into the war. This forced Britain to send soldiers to the West Indies and Europe, leaving them fewer soldiers to take back the colonies. It also provided the Americans with French troops. Britain could no longer bring their full might against the Americans, and the Americans had help.

Valley Forge (Encampment)

It was difficult to fight during the winter. In December 1777, George Washington and his army encamped at Valley Forge to wait out the winter. They even built log cabins in which to shelter. Washington's army suffered a terrible supply crisis while trying to retrain and reorganize the army to counter British attacks. Many soldiers died from disease, malnutrition (starvation), as well as the cold and wet weather.

The suffering endured during this time became a cultural legend and an important piece of history for many decades.

The Battle of Yorktown (British Surrender at Yorktown)

In September and October 1781, George Washington and his army, as well as French soldiers and navy, attacked and defeated the British army at Yorktown. New artillery and naval bombardment were key factors that weakened British defenses. More importantly, malaria was rampant in the area. The British general estimated that half of his soldiers were suffering from the disease and unable to fight.

This was the last major battle of the American Revolutionary War. The British could no longer withstand the extensive and expensive campaign, especially while dealing with the French and Spanish, with whom they were also at war. The American victory finally prompted the British government to begin negotiations to end the conflict.

The End of the American Revolution

The Treaty of Paris was signed in 1783, ending the American Revolution and giving the colonies independence.

After the war, the Constitution of the United States was written in 1787, creating a new nation.

Women of the Revolution

Women played many important roles during the war. Even as armies marched, they were followed by thousands of women who provided vital goods and services and who maintained hospitals and camps. Without these critical support roles, American armies would have been far less able and successful.

Some women dressed up as men to become soldiers including: Anna Maria Lane, Sybil Ludington, and Sally St. Clair. Nancy Hart single-handedly captured six enemy soldiers when they stormed into her home to ransack it.

African Americans During the Revolution

During the time of the war, there were about 500,000 slaves in the colonies, mostly on southern plantations. Some were promised freedom if they bore arms and fought. As the war carried on, more and more British units included African Americans as regular soldiers.

Between 25,000 and 50,000 served the British army. About 5,000 served the American Continental Army. While George Washington convinced Congress to allow African Americans to serve as soldiers, he also tried to return them to slavery after the war. After the Battle of Yorktown and defeat, the British refused to allow Black soldiers to be made slaves again, and 8,000 to 10,000 freed blacks were evacuated to London, UK; 3,000 to 4,000 to Nova Scotia, Canada; and, about 15,000 to Jamaica and the Bahamas.

American Indians During the War

Most Indigenous people were against the formation of an American nation because it threatened their territory and people. About 13,000 fought for the British. This alliance would lead to decades of conflict with the U.S.A after the war.

Indigenous peoples were not included in peace negotiations, the Treaty of Paris, or the formation of the new nation.

78. Who wrote the Declaration of Independence? *

- *(Thomas) Jefferson*

The Declaration of Independence

The thirteen original colonies that would eventually become states were: New Hampshire, Massachusetts, Rhode Island, Connecticut, New York, New Jersey, Pennsylvania, Delaware, Maryland, Virginia, North Carolina, South Carolina, and Georgia.

During the summer of 1776, delegates from the colonies met

in Philadelphia to discuss freedom from England. Some delegates wanted to convince the people that it was time for the colonies to be free from England. However, not all the Representatives were in favor of such a radical move. This was a chance for everyone to agree on a shared plan for the future.

Throughout the 1760s and 1770s, people in the American colonies increasingly felt like Britain's way of governing them was a burden and unfair. They wanted their own government.

In 1776, a committee was appointed and tasked with drafting a document that outlined why the thirteen American colonies wished to break free from British governance.

The committee of five people consisted of: John Adams, Thomas Jefferson, Benjamin Franklin, Robert Livingston, and Roger Sherman.

John Adams appointed Thomas Jefferson, age thirty-three, to be the leading writer of the Declaration of Independence because he felt that Jefferson was popular, a good writer, and an influential Virginian delegate.

It took Jefferson seventeen days to write the document. Finally, he showed it to Congress on June 28, 1776, and they decided to go forward on July 2.

Thomas Jefferson

Thomas Jefferson (1743–1826) was one of the Founding Fathers of the United States of America. After writing the Declaration of Independence, and following the successful American Revolutionary War, he became the first U.S. Secretary of State under America's first president, George Washington, and the second vice president under the second president, John Adams. He then became the third president, serving from 1801–1809.

As president, Jefferson fought against pirates in the Barbary Wars and resisted British trade policies. He oversaw the purchase of the Louisiana territory from France, which included most of what is now the middle of the continental U.S.A, and which doubled the size of

America at the time. He also supported the famous Lewis and Clark Expedition, which explored the American interior and northwest.

Jefferson was a lover of books. In his youth, he collected two hundred books for a personal library, which was a very large amount at the time. When this library was destroyed by a fire, he embarked on building a second, acquiring nearly 6,500 books. When the Library of Congress burned down, Jefferson sold his collection to the U.S. government to help rebuild. He then started his third private collection, reaching almost 2,000 books at the time of his death.

Jefferson was a strong proponent of religious freedom and wrote the Virginia Statute for Religious Freedom. He also dreamed of a university that was completely separate from religious influence. In 1819, he founded the University of Virginia, designed its first buildings (including America's first observatory), planned the school's curriculum, and served as the first head of the school. He left most of his final book collection to the library when he died.

Jefferson passed away on July 4, 1826, on the fiftieth anniversary of the Declaration of Independence. Fellow Founding Father, and longtime friend and political rival, John Adams, passed away the same day.

The Motto of the United States

The nation's first motto was *E pluribus unum*. It means, *We all became one* or *Out of Many, One*. The motto was proposed by Thomas Jefferson, Benjamin Franklin, and John Adams in 1776 for the first Great Seal of the United States. It serves as a reminder that America was able to make one nation out of a collection of states and many people from different backgrounds and beliefs.

The modern motto of the United States, however, is, *In God We Trust*. The phrase first appeared on U.S. coins in 1864 and was made official in 1956 at the height of the Cold War to signal opposition to the ideology of communism.

79. When was the Declaration of Independence adopted?

- *July 4, 1776*

After the document was edited, the Declaration of Independence was ratified and adopted on July 4, 1776.

Creating and signing the document was serious business. Simply signing this document was considered high treason against the British Crown, a crime punishable by torture and death.

The Declaration of Independence is referred to as the document responsible for the birth of the United States of America. It announced a new nation and a new beginning. Every year, Americans still celebrate Independence Day on July 4 as a holiday.

80. The American Revolution had many important events. Name one.

- *(Battle of) Bunker Hill – see page 105*
- *Declaration of Independence – see page 108*
- *Washington Crossing the Delaware (Battle of Trenton) – see page 105*
- *(Battle of) Saratoga – see page 106*
- *Valley Forge (Encampment) – see page 106*
- *(Battle of) Yorktown (British surrender at Yorktown) – see page 107*

81. There were 13 original states. Name five.

- *New Hampshire*
- *Massachusetts*
- *Rhode Island*
- *Connecticut*

- *New York*
- *New Jersey*
- *Pennsylvania*
- *Delaware*
- *Maryland*
- *Virginia*
- *North Carolina*
- *South Carolina*
- *Georgia*

The most populous state at this time was Virginia with 690,000 people (including 288,000 slaves). Pennsylvania had 430,000 people (including 3,700 slaves). Massachusetts had 378,000 people and was the only state with no slaves.

The thirteen states occupied only a small portion of North America. Most of the territory was colonized by Britain (Canada) and Spain (Mexico, middle America and the Southwest, and the entire Pacific coast).

82. What founding document was written in 1787?

- *(U.S.) Constitution*

The Constitutional Convention

On May 25, 1787, fifty-five delegates from the different states of the United States met at the Pennsylvania State House in Philadelphia to establish a "more perfect union" between states.

The delegates mainly consisted of wealthy men, men with college degrees, and landowners. Out of the thirteen states, twelve were represented. Rhode Island was not in favor of a powerful central government. They saw the gathering as an effort to overthrow its government's current working, so the state did not send a representative.

George Washington was unanimously elected to preside over the Constitutional Convention. It started a series of secret meetings where only the delegates present had an idea of what was said.

James Madison was elected to keep minutes, but these were kept private for many years. The meetings were so secret that the Founding Fathers hired guards to prohibit curious bystanders from entering. Reporters wished they could enter, but the security was sound. The meetings lasted over a period of about three months.

The U.S. Constitution eventually resulted from a conglomeration of ideas. Documents that influenced the final Constitution included: the Mayflower Compact, the Iroquois Great Law of Peace, the Fundamental Orders of Connecticut, the Virginia Declaration of Rights, the Federalist Papers, the Anti-Federalist Papers, the Virginia Plan, and the New Jersey Plan.

The Virginia Declaration of Rights

The Virginia Declaration of Rights emphasized the protection of individual rights, and it was the first declaration of rights that called for a free press.

Section 1 of the Virginia Declaration said that "all men are *by nature equally free* and have inherent rights." Section 2 cemented people as the source of all power, and Section 3 noted that the people could replace governments if the latter did not meet their needs. Section 4 said that no one could inherit power, and Section 5 proclaimed the separation of political powers.

Later, the Virginia Declaration would influence the Declaration of Independence, and many of these rights would subsequently also be incorporated into the U.S. Bill of Rights.

The Fundamental Orders of Connecticut

The Fundamental Orders of Connecticut relied on the philosophy of Reverend Thomas Hooker and supported the idea of the consent of the governed. The concept impressed Thomas Jefferson so much that he inserted this idea later in the Declaration of Independence.

In 1637, political leaders created a general court that could rule over Hartford, Windsor, and Wethersfield. They agreed that the framework for the government should be in writing and approved by the public. Eventually, the Fundamental Orders of Connecticut came to be, stating the powers and the limits of the government. The eleven orders gave men voting rights and allowed more people to run for office. The orders also called for general court sessions twice a year and limited how long a person could be governor.

General courts got executive, legislative, and judicial authority through this document.

The Mayflower Compact

The Mayflower Compact was a document signed on the old and crowded pilgrim ship, the *Mayflower*, on November 21, 1620, just before the ship's landing in Plymouth, Massachusetts.

People living in Leyden, Holland wanted to come to America. In 1619, they got a patent from the Virginia Company to start a private plantation. The *Mayflower* pilgrims set sail in September 1620 and were joined by more people from London. These people were not under the original jurisdiction of the Virginia Company.

The *Mayflower* had intended to anchor near the Hudson River, but rough seas prevented it. Instead, the captain steered the ship toward Cape Cod, and the passengers were now no longer within the jurisdiction of the charter granted to them by the Virginia Company in England.

Friction arose because the pilgrims were uncertain about what to do. Pilgrim leaders drafted the Mayflower Compact before even going ashore in order to preserve unity and to establish some form of government to keep the "undesirable lot" from London under control. The Mayflower Compact was not intended to be a constitution, but rather a temporary substitute for a charter. The Compact was remarkable because it was written by people who were essentially equal to each other and looking for ways for all of them to live together peacefully.

The short document bound the signatories to form a government upon landing and pledged them to abide by shared laws and regulations.

The Mayflower Compact proved to be a provisional instrument focusing on common consent and self-government, which later became the foundation of the Plymouth government. Scholars interpret it as an essential step in the evolution of democratic America.

The Iroquois Great Law of Peace

The Indigenous peoples of the Iroquois Confederacy were a society of over five thousand people when the first European explorers encountered them during the seventeenth century.

Initially, these people lived as five different tribes, sometimes in conflict. The cost of war was high and weakened their society. The Great Peacemaker was sent by the Creator and together with Hiawatha, chief of the Onondaga tribe, they suggested a great law of peace and united the five nations into one in the twelfth or thirteenth century. The Tuscarora joined in 1722 to establish what is now known as the Six Nations. Each nation maintained its own leadership, but jointly discussed common ground at the Great Council of Chiefs.

The concept was based on consensus and peace rather than fighting. The Iroquois Confederacy is the oldest living participatory democracy on Earth, and many of the democratic principles of that political system found their way into the U.S. Constitution.

For instance, the Iroquois Confederacy already had methods to remove leaders from the Confederacy (which would become Article II, Section 4 in the Constitution). They also had a clause that delineated who had the power to declare war (which would become Article I, Section 8 in the Constitution).

Additional Influences

THE VIRGINIA PLAN

At the start of the Constitutional Convention, The Virginia Plan was presented by a state governor Edmund Jennings Randolph. He was the delegate from the state of Virginia.

The Virginia Plan suggested a framework that could serve as the blueprint for the new Constitution. The plan proposed that all states be represented in the government according to their population. It also suggested that the government be divided into three branches—executive, judicial, and legislative – thus creating a national government. The idea was to create a more powerful government, but by dividing it into branches, no single branch would have too much power.

George Washington (who was from Virginia) fully supported the plan, and it set the tone for the creation of the Constitution.

THE NEW JERSEY PLAN

Not everyone was ready to accept the Virginia Plan. For New Jersey, ideas about representation provided a problem.

The New Jersey Plan, proposed by William Peterson, said that the government must protect smaller states. If representation were to be determined by population, smaller states would be disadvantaged. New Jersey specifically was not categorized as a so-called slave state. They felt representation by population was unfair, as the slave population in other states would contribute to a higher population count, thus increasing representation in Congress.

The New Jersey Plan aimed to curb the power of the largest states and protect the smaller states. It proposed that each state should have only one vote in Congress.

83. The Federalist Papers supported the passage of the U.S. Constitution. Name <u>one</u> of the writers.

- *(James) Madison*
- *(Alexander) Hamilton*
- *(John) Jay*
- *Publius*

The Federalist Papers

The Federalist Papers were written by statesmen Alexander Hamilton, James Madison, and John Jay, but the work appeared anonymously under the penname Publius in New York newspapers between 1787 and 1788. Initially a series of eighty-five serial essays, the papers advised people to ratify the new U.S. Constitution. The pieces told them that the new Constitution would not threaten public liberty.

The authors argued that decentralization of power was not the way to go for the new American nation. The Federalist papers explained the key provisions of what should be contained in the new Constitution and how this republican form of government could work.

84. Why were the Federalist Papers important?

- *They helped people understand the (U.S.) Constitution*
- *They supported passing the (U.S.) Constitution*

The Anti-Federalist Papers

Eight days after the Constitution's final draft was written, some Founding Fathers started publishing a series of essays arguing *against* the proposed new Constitution. Called the Anti-Federalist Papers, these works opposed a more powerful central government.

Although the Anti-Federalist Papers were not as influential as the

Federalist Papers, they nevertheless helped shape the early American political landscape, and eventually, the passage of the U.S. Bill of Rights.

The Anti-Federalist Papers were written during the course of a few years under the pseudonym Brutus, and many writers contributed. Generally speaking, the Anti-Federalist Papers feared a strong central government, as well as wealthy merchants and industrialists who could influence the government improperly. The writers also believed that direct citizen participation was necessary for a democracy.

James Madison

A federalist at heart, James Madison is described as being the "Father of the Constitution." He was elected the fourth president of the U.S.A in 1808.

He was the most influential of all Founding Fathers, with his plan to divide the government into three branches: the executive, the judicial, and the legislative branches. He was also a co-writer on the Federalist Papers and the Bill of Rights.

James Madison was Princeton's original graduate student. He went to the College of New Jersey (now Princeton University) at age eighteen and blazed through a four-year course in just two years, often sleeping only four hours per night. He studied law, Greek and Roman philosophy, the Hebrew language, and more.

Alexander Hamilton

Alexander Hamilton's birthdate is unknown, but he was not born in the U.S. Hamilton called the island of Nevis in the Leeward Islands (then part of the British West Indian colonies) home during his early years.

He was the founding member of the Federalist Party, the first opposing political party in American history. Together with James Madison and John Jay, Hamilton wrote the Federalist Papers, a collection of eighty-five essays that did a lot to persuade the states to ratify the newly drafted Constitution.

Alexander Hamilton founded The New York Post. First called *The New*

York Evening Post, the newspaper came into being in November 1801. The publication was an anti-Democratic/Republican leaning publication that regularly slandered Thomas Jefferson.

Hamilton was the U.S.'s first Secretary of the Treasury, and he helped establish the First Bank of the United States.

John Jay

John Jay was a founder of the U.S. He was a lawyer, the first chief justice of the U.S. (where he had only four cases over six years), and the second Governor of New York. He was an important leader of the Federalist Party, believing in a strong central government.

While Jay was Governor of New York, Alexander Hamilton sent him a letter asking him to gerrymander New York for the presidential election of 1796. That is, Hamilton wanted Jay to redraw district lines to manipulate the election's results. Jay refused.

85. Benjamin Franklin is famous for many things. Name one.

- *Founded the first free public libraries*
- *First Postmaster General of the United States*
- *Helped write the Declaration of Independence*
- *Inventor*
- *U.S. diplomat*

French Support for American Independence

Benjamin Franklin was an American diplomat with a magnetic personality. To gain European support for American independence, he went to France from 1776 to 1778. His presence in France annoyed the British enormously.

Eventually, Benjamin Franklin's popularity, his diplomatic skill, and the American military at Saratoga convinced France to recognize

America as an independent nation and to formally ally with the thirteen states. Supporting America was a way for France to get back at Britain after losing North American territory to Britain in the Seven Years' War (also known in North America as the French and Indian War).

On February 6, 1778, the Treaty of Alliance and the Treaty of Amity and Commerce were signed between America and France. The Treaty of Alliance stated that both countries would help each other if either was attacked by Britain. Neither of the two countries could seek a separate peace agreement with Britain. The Treaty of Amity and Commerce promoted commercial ties and trade between France and America.

The French supplied military aid to America, which turned out to be fundamental in the fight against Britain. Benjamin Franklin was made the permanent American ambassador to France.

Considered one of the most brilliant Americans of his age, Benjamin Franklin did not go to school for very long. By age twelve, he was already working in his brother's printing shop. However, he loved books and often went without food to afford new volumes. He founded the first free public libraries within the U.S. Franklin was also a scientist, author, and inventor. He helped write the Declaration of Independence.

Benjamin Franklin was the only Founding Father who signed all four of the key documents that led to the formation of the United States: the Declaration of Independence, the Treaty of Alliance with France, the peace treaty with Britain in 1783, and the U.S. Constitution. He signed the Constitution at age eighty-one.

Benjamin Franklin created a phonetic alphabet because he was annoyed about the inconsistencies in English spelling. He ditched C, J, Q, W, X, and Y in his version and created new letters to represent new vocal sounds. His phonetic alphabet was unveiled in 1779 but failed to capture the public's attention.

86. George Washington is famous for many things. Name one.*

- *"Father of Our Country"*
- *First president of the United States*
- *General of the Continental Army*
- *President of the Constitutional Convention*

George Washington

> *His features are regular and placid with all the muscles of his face in perfect control, though flexible and expressive of deep feelings when moved by emotions. In conversation, he looks you full in the face, is deliberate, deferential, and engaging. His demeanor at all times composed and dignified. His movements and gestures are graceful, his walk majestic and he is a splendid horseman.*
>
> —George Washington, through the eyes of his aide, Captain George Mercer, 1790.

The Father of America was raised in colonial Virginia. George Washington was the son of a prosperous planter. During the American Revolution, he became a national hero when he led the colonial forces to victory over the British as the Continental Army General.

After being Commander in Chief for the Continental Army, George Washington became the first American president in 1789. When the president's job description was outlined in Article II of the U.S. Constitution, it was written with Washington in mind, and he was unopposed in his run for office. He served two terms. Washington was the only president ever to be elected unanimously.

Washington realized that how he handled being president would set a precedent for the future, so he set out to create a legacy. He worked out treaty creation procedures, decided how advisors to the president should act, and established the tradition of a State of the Union speech every year. He created banks and appointed federal judges. He worked hard to keep his new country out of wars.

After serving two terms, President George Washington stepped down from his position. He felt it was important for a president not to act like a king and rule too long. There had to be room for new ideas. George Washington died in 1799 from a bad cold and a throat infection. He died just three years after leaving office, at age sixty-seven.

Figure 8: © Shutterstock / bigwa11, used under license

Washington's legacy shows the American people that prosperity and hope for the future can lie in a strong union under a central authority. Because his ideas have stood the test of time, George Washington is widely honored for building the foundations of a powerful national government.

Father of the U.S. Military

When Washington died, he had been a lieutenant general. However, some felt that this three-star rank did not do justice to what this great man accomplished, having achieved many important victories during the American Revolution. Not only did he defeat the British in battle, but he also established the framework of how American soldiers should behave and relate to others.

George Washington set a precedent with almost every decision he made. Some called him the "Father of the U.S. Military."

In 1976, George Washington was posthumously awarded the

U.S. military title of General of the Armies of the United States. No one in history will ever be able to rank higher than him.

Slavery

All his life, George Washington had a complicated relationship with slavery. He grew up with slaves and inherited his own slaves when his father died in 1743. When he got married, his wife, Martha, brought her slaves to the household.

Over the years, George became more uncomfortable with the thought of owning other human beings. However, although he supported abolition in theory, he needed slaves to work as laborers on his plantation. At last, in his will, he freed his slaves with the stipulation that they must remain with his wife for the rest of her life.

87. Thomas Jefferson is famous for many things. Name one.

- *Writer of the Declaration of Independence*
- *Third president of the United States*
- *Doubled the size of the United States (Louisiana Purchase)*
- *First Secretary of State*
- *Founded the University of Virginia*
- *Writer of the Virginia Statute on Religious Freedom*

88. James Madison is famous for many things. Name one.

- *"Father of the Constitution"*
- *Fourth president of the United States*
- *President during the War of 1812*

- *One of the writers of the Federalist Papers*

89. Alexander Hamilton is famous for many things. Name one.

- *First Secretary of the Treasury*
- *One of the writers of the Federalist Papers*
- *Helped establish the First Bank of the United States*
- *Aide to General George Washington*
- *Member of the Continental Congress*

QUESTIONS 89-99: 1800S

America During the 1800s

During the 1800s, the American social and economic landscape changed significantly. Farms and plantations spread westward, and coastal cities grew. Population boomed, and immigrants from Germany, Scotland, and Ireland poured into the new nation, adding diversity to the American states.

Trade between the states grew, and ships traveled the American coastline almost as frequently as they sailed to Europe or the Caribbean islands. There were regional differences, but the people of America continued to share many experiences.

In 1803, the United States bought the Louisiana Territory from France.

In 1845, America annexed Texas, which Mexico considered its territory, leading to the Mexican-American War. The U.S. won the war, gaining Texas, California, Nevada, and Utah, as well as parts of Arizona, Colorado, New Mexico, and Wyoming.

The addition of so much new territory upset the balance between states that were for or against the use of slaves. This was a factor leading to the U.S. Civil War.

90. What territory did the United States buy from France in 1803?

- *Louisiana Territory*
- *Louisiana*

The Louisiana Purchase

In 1682, the Kingdom of France took control of the Louisiana territory. It was then ceded to Spain in 1762. France's Napoleon Bonaparte, of the then-new French Republic, took control of Louisiana in 1800.

U.S. President Thomas Jefferson was long interested in acquiring the region and gaining control of the Mississippi River and the port of New Orleans. When the Americans asked, France was eager to sell. The offering price was $15 million ($424.5 million in 2025 dollars).

The Louisiana territory would double the size of the young nation. At the time, Louisiana's non-Indigenous population was about 60,000 people, about half of them slaves, as well as many French speakers who would bring a significant addition to the cultural landscape of America.

At no point did any European power consider Indigenous Americans when they bought and sold and decided who owned the Louisiana territory, despite the fact many tribes existed in the area. For forty years after the purchase, a series of court decisions removed various tribes for resettlement, culminating in the Trail of Tears. It spawned the idea of Indigenous land rights, which has persisted until today. Restitution, land control, and other issues remain an important discussion for all Americans.

91. Name <u>one</u> war fought by the United States in the 1800s.

- *War of 1812*
- *Mexican-American War*
- *Civil War*
- *Spanish-American War*

The War of 1812

War had raged between Great Britain and France since 1803. Canada, under British rule at that time, was the battleground. America, wanting to be neutral, kept up communication and trade with both France and Britain.

In 1806, France passed a law prohibiting trade between neutral parties, such as the U.S. and Britain. Britain retaliated, passing the same law, making any trade between France and the U.S. unlawful. While trying to hurt each other, the two countries also hurt the U.S. The U.S. objected.

Britain rejected America's claim that they were neutral, dismissing their legitimacy as a country. They abducted American sailors at sea, forcing them into the Royal Navy against their will. Britain also armed Native Americans so that they could prey on frontier settlers. America suffered.

The conflict climaxed on June 22, 1807 when *Leopard*, a British warship, stopped the American ship, the *Chesapeake*. The British were looking for three deserters and wanted to search the American boat. When the *Chesapeake*'s commander refused, shots were fired, and three people were killed. The Americans had to surrender, and the British boarded the ship, finding only one British citizen.

America was furious, and the Embargo Act was passed on December 22, 1807. It prohibited American ships from trading in all foreign ports. President Thomas Jefferson did not want war, but he tried to hit France and Britain where it hurt: their economies.

The act did not affect Britain or France that much, but it damaged the American economy. In 1809, Congress replaced the Embargo Act with the Non-Intercourse Act, which continued to put pressure on Britain and France, but loosened restrictions on American trade. The U.S. could now trade with other European nations, as long as they were not France or Britain.

The Macon Bill of 1810 superseded the Non-Intercourse Act. The act stated that if either France or Britain agreed to support the neutrality of the U.S., America would resume trading with that country while not trading with the other. Napoleon wanted to make trouble for Britain and agreed to the terms. The U.S. reinstated trade restrictions on Britain and began thinking about formal war.

Eventually, on June 18, 1812, the U.S. formally declared war against Britain, both to redress grievances and to claim Canada for themselves. Ironically, the British Parliament had been planning to lift the trade restrictions against the U.S., and it did so soon after the U.S. declared war. Even though one of the leading causes for the war was gone, fighting began anyway.

The War of 1812 was fought in merchant shipping lanes along the U.S.'s Atlantic coast, along the Great Lakes and the Saint Lawrence River, and along the coast of the Gulf of Mexico.

America was vastly outnumbered by the British, so they resorted to a different strategy instead of direct engagement. The U.S. invaded Canada during the summer of 1812 and tried to force the British to the negotiating table by using Canada as a bargaining chip. The plan failed. The British army was too strong for the U.S. forces.

In September 1813, the U.S. Navy destroyed a British fleet on Lake Erie. This was one of the U.S.'s few victories.

In August 1814, in retaliation for the Americans brutally burning and looting York (now Toronto) in Upper Canada, British troops from Canada burned Washington, D.C. including the Capitol and the White House. President Madison's wife, Dolley Madison, managed to save many records and treasures before the British arrived.

President Madison and other officials had mistakenly believed in an easy victory and prepared for a feast. When this assumption proved wrong, they quickly fled the city. When troops arrived at the White House, they ate the dinner left for the President and drank his wine.

On December 24, 1814, representatives of America and Britain met in Ghent in Belgium and signed the Treaty of Ghent, which ended the war. One historical writer called it an "actual sigh of relief" for both countries. Unfortunately, 15,000 Americans had lost their lives.

While Americans later portrayed the war in heroic terms, in other nations it was seen as a very wasteful conflict with unnecessary losses, and a triumph against American aggression.

In terms of the treaty, all lands reverted to their original owners, the way things had been before the war. Ironically, relations between the warring countries improved after everything was over.

The Mexican-American War

In 1845, the U.S. one-sidedly annexed Texas, which Mexico refused to recognize. In 1846, the U.S. invaded Mexico. The U.S. Navy blockaded Baja, California and sent soldiers through the port of Veracruz so that the U.S. could capture Mexico City.

Mexico was defeated, but peace was difficult to negotiate. The war caused great turmoil in Mexico, as well as extensive loss of life. Mexico lost half of its territory, and its economy was shattered.

In the end, the U.S. gained present-day Texas, California, Nevada, Utah, and parts of Arizona, Colorado, New Mexico, and Wyoming. The U.S also agreed to pay $15 million ($631.22 million in 2025 dollars) in damages. The war set the border between the U.S. and Mexico as the Rio Grande river.

With this new territory, the U.S. now stretched from coast to coast across the continent.

The Civil War

See Question 92 for more information.

The Spanish-American War

The United States had been interested in Cuba, a Spanish colony, for a long time. By 1898, the U.S. had more than $50 million invested in Cuba, and annual trade in sugar was worth much more.

At one point, Spanish rulers started to move the Cuban population into centralized locations guarded by Spanish troops. The people were unhappy with this and rebelled. As a result, the entire country went under martial law in February 1896.

The U.S. supported the independence of Cuba because it would be economically beneficial. The Spanish-American War started on April 25, 1898, when the U.S. declared war against Spain. The conflict lasted for three months. The war ended with an American victory.

As a result of the war, Cuba gained independence, and Spain gave up control of the Philippines, Guam, and Puerto Rico to the U.S. for $20 million. The total cost of the war to the United States was $250 million and three thousand lives.

92. Name the U.S. war between the North and the South.

- *The Civil War*

The Civil War

The end of the War of 1812 resulted in an era of growth in American cities and industries. Before the war, the U.S. had been primarily agricultural, and most of the population had lived in rural areas. However, the Industrial Revolution that had been taking place in Britain now spilled over to North America. Immigrants came from Europe and Asia, and the population increased. As a result, the U.S. economy exploded.

Slavery formed the backbone of the agricultural economy in

southern U.S. states, whereas the northern states were more industry-driven, and slavery was far less common. Although many believed slavery to be wrong, the practice continued through the first half of the nineteenth century.

The South wanted slaves on their plantations and in their houses as cheap labor. The North wanted to set the slaves free because of the horrible conditions they suffered. Most northerners believed that non-white people were inferior to white people, but they could not support the inhumane conditions the slaves endured.

Politicians on both sides tried to find a compromise but failed. As a result, eleven southern states left the United States Union and formed the Confederate States of America: South Carolina, Mississippi, Florida, Alabama, Georgia, Louisiana, Texas, Virginia, Arkansas, North Carolina, and Tennessee.

The North and South continued to find conflict with each other. In 1861, the Civil War erupted. The Civil War was the deadliest war in American history up to that date and lasted until 1865.

The Battle of Fort Sumter

The Battle of Fort Sumter was the battle that started the American Civil War. The North and South fought over two days in April 1861. Fort Sumter was on an island, and its purpose was to guard Charleston Harbor. After thirty-four hours of battle, Union soldiers (the North) had to surrender the fort when their ammunition ran out. The only casualties were two Union soldiers, who died when a cannon exploded.

Confederate troops (the Confederacy, or the South) then occupied the fort for the next four years, standing their ground against Union soldiers. They only abandoned it just before the capture of Charleston by William T. Sherman in February 1865.

As the war began, states that had not yet picked a side now had to side with either the North or the South.

President Lincoln of the North initially believed that the war would be short and limited. Therefore, he called for seventy-five thousand volunteers to serve for three months.

Unfortunately, the Civil War lasted for four years, and 2 million men fought as part of the Union Army.

The Battle of Gettysburg

The Confederate Army was outnumbered in many ways but scored occasional victories over the Union soldiers. Confederate General, Robert E. Lee, thought a decisive win might clinch things in their favor. He began marching north with his men in June 1863 and eventually engaged in battle with the Union.

General Lee attacked aggressively and lost over half of his soldiers, forcing him to retreat. The Battle of Gettysburg was the deadliest battle of the Civil War. Twenty-three thousand Union soldiers and twenty-eight thousand Confederates were killed, wounded, or captured over just three days from July 1–3, 1863. Although the war went on for two more years, many historians say that Gettysburg was the turning point toward the final Union victory.

Although the Battle of Gettysburg ended in early July 1863, President Abraham Lincoln delivered the Gettysburg Address over four months later, on November 19, 1863, at the dedication of the Soldiers' National Cemetery. The speech lasted just two minutes, yet it is now considered one of the greatest speeches ever delivered in the English language.

> *We met on a great battlefield of the war. We have come to indicate a portion of that field as a final resting place for those who here gave their lives that a nation might live.*
>
> —Lincoln, from the Gettysburg Address.

The Battle of Antietam/Sharpsburg

The Battle of Antietam is, to this day, the deadliest one-day battle in American history.

Confederate General, Robert E. Lee, of the South wanted to move the battleground from the South to the North. Victories in the North by the Confederates could influence upcoming elections and perhaps also persuade European nations to recognize the Confederacy as a new nation.

The Battle of Antietam (also called the Battle of Sharpsburg) took place on September 17, 1862 near the Antietam Creek in Maryland. It was fought in a narrow field between the creek and the Potomac River. Five thousand men died, and another eighteen thousand were wounded in a mere eight hours. The North won.

The outcome of the battle proved that the Union could hold its own against the Confederate Army. This gave President Lincoln confidence to issue the Emancipation Proclamation from a position of strength.

Although historians now say the battle was a stalemate, the Union claimed victory at the time. This ended the Confederate hope that Great Britain and France would acknowledge their struggle and come to their aid. Consequently, the Confederates were isolated, and it was harder for them to resupply. This battle may have turned the whole course of the Civil War in favor of the Union.

Lincoln's Assassination

Initially, Confederate sympathizer John Wilkes Booth and other co-conspirators planned to kidnap the president and take him to the Confederate capital as a hostage to end the Civil War. But in late March, on the day of the planned kidnapping, President Lincoln did not appear at the spot where the conspirators had lain in wait.

Two weeks later, Confederate General Robert E. Lee surrendered at Appomattox. Booth became desperate to save the Confederacy.

Learning that Lincoln planned to go to Ford's Theatre on April 14, Booth masterminded a new plan. He entered the state box where Lincoln was sitting and shot him in the back of the head. Lincoln died early the following morning on April 15. He was fifty-six years old.

Booth was apprehended on April 26 and shot in the neck. His last words were, "Useless. Useless," which he uttered while staring at his hands. His co-conspirators were later convicted and executed by hanging on July 7, 1865.

The End of the Civil War

The last battle of the Civil War was fought in Texas at the Palmito Ranch on May 13, 1865.

Surrender terms were signed on June 2, 1865 by Confederate General, Edmund Kirby Smith, bringing an end to the bloodiest four years in U.S. history up to that date.

As several Confederate commanders had yet to capitulate, the new president, Andrew Johnson, could not formally declare the war over until August 20, 1866.

93. The Civil War had many important events. Name one.

- *(Battle of) Fort Sumter– see page 131*
- *Emancipation Proclamation– see page 137*
- *(Battle of) Vicksburg*
- *(Battle of) Gettysburg– see page 132*
- *Sherman's March*
- *(Surrender at) Appomattox– see page 133*
- *(Battle of) Antietam/Sharpsburg– see page 133*
- *Lincoln was assassinated– see page 133*

Origins of the Civil War

Slavery was very prevalent in the Southern states due to the number of people needed to work cotton plantations. Owners made more money with cheap slaves rather than paying regular workers. If they lost the slaves, and lost their cheap labor, they could not continue to be rich and powerful. That made them very motivated to fight to keep slavery legal. They believed that slavery was a state right and the federal government could not take it away from them.

However, in the North, more and more people were against slavery. When Abraham Lincoln won the 1860 presidential election, Southern leaders panicked, sure he would try to end slavery. Seven slave states (South Carolina, Mississippi, Florida, Alabama, Georgia, Louisiana, and Texas) declared that they would leave (secede) from the U.S. However, this would greatly weaken the young nation, both economically and militarily. Each smaller nation would be helpless in the face of world powers. Formal secession was refused.

The slave states seceded, anyway and prepared for war. Without warning, they seized multiple U.S. forts, beginning with the Battle of Fort Sumter.

94. Abraham Lincoln is famous for many things. Name one. *

- *Freed the slaves (Emancipation Proclamation)*
- *Saved (or preserved) the Union*
- *Led the United States during the Civil War*
- *16th president of the United States*
- *Delivered the Gettysburg Addressr*

Abraham Lincoln

As the sixteenth American president and a self-educated leader, Abraham Lincoln's presidency was overshadowed by the American Civil War.

From the beginning, Lincoln was very clear about his opposition to slavery. The Southern states feared that he would abolish slavery, so several left the U.S. (Union) to form the Confederate States of America (Confederacy). Lincoln was stoic in his stance that the Union had to be preserved, even if it meant war. Abraham Lincoln became president in 1860, shortly before the outbreak of the Civil War.

Lincoln proved to be a great leader and a shrewd strategist, which helped preserve the Union and led them to victory in the war. The Emancipation Proclamation paved the way for abolishing slavery, while his Gettysburg Address still stands as one of the most famous speeches in American history.

Unfortunately, with the Union on the brink of victory in the Civil War, Abraham Lincoln was assassinated by a Confederate sympathizer in April 1865.

The Wrestler

As a young man, Abraham Lincoln was an accomplished wrestler. In about three hundred matches, he was defeated only once. As a result, Lincoln was honored in the National Wrestling Hall of Fame as an 'Outstanding American.'

95. What did the Emancipation Proclamation do?

- *Freed the slaves*
- *Freed slaves in the Confederacy*
- *Freed slaves in the Confederate states*
- *Freed slaves in most Southern states*

96. What U.S. war ended slavery?

- *The Civil War*

The Emancipation Proclamation

The Emancipation Proclamation was an order issued by President Abraham Lincoln to free slaves in the U.S. during the American Civil War. It was a war order that overrode the power of states to decide their own laws regarding slavery.

Figure 9: © Shutterstock / Ntguilty, used under license

Figure 10: Emancipation Proclamation, public domain, National Archives

The Confederacy controlled ten states, so their slaves were not immediately freed. Slaves in the North were freed. During the war, about 4 million slaves were freed as the Union Army advanced into Confederate states. Some of the slaves even joined the Union Army.

The Emancipation Proclamation stated that the ending of slavery was a goal of the Civil War. However, although many slaves were freed, the proclamation did not make slavery illegal. This only happened with the passing of the Thirteenth Amendment of the U.S. Constitution, which declared slavery illegal everywhere in the United States.

97. What amendment says all persons born or naturalized in the United States, and subject to the jurisdiction thereof, are U.S. citizens?

- *14th Amendment*

The 14th Amendment states that the States must treat individuals equally and follow a fair process before depriving them of life, liberty, or property.

98. When did all men get the right to vote?

- *After the Civil War*
- *During Reconstruction*
- *(With the) 15th Amendment*
- *1870*

99. Name one leader of the women's rights movement in the 1800s.

- *Susan B. Anthony*
- *Elizabeth Cady Stanton*
- *Sojourner Truth*
- *Harriet Tubman*
- *Lucretia Mott*
- *Lucy Stone*

Susan B. Anthony

Susan B. Anthony was an important figure in the women's suffrage and anti-slavery movements. She travelled all over and gave 75–100 speeches a year, as well as supported many political campaigns. She even worked internationally, helping found the International Council of Women, which is still active today.

Figure 11: © Shutterstock / Everett Collection, used under license

In the beginning, she was accused of trying to destroy the institution of marriage, and people publicly hated and abused her, but during her own lifetime, that public sentiment completely reversed. On her 80th birthday, President William McKinley celebrated her at the White House; she had grown into a revered figure. She was the first woman to appear on U.S. coinage, the 1979 dollar.

During the Civil War, Anthony and others founded the Women's Loyal National League and conducted the largest petition drive the U.S. had ever seen before. They collected four hundred thousand signatures in support of ending slavery. This was at a time long before phones and Internet, the population of the U.S. was much smaller, and it was wartime. To collect so many signatures was a monumental achievement.

In 1872, Anthony illegally voted in an election in which only men were allowed to vote. Her trial was widely publicized and led to a conviction and a fine, which she refused to pay. In 1878, Anthony and Elizabeth Cady Stanton presented Congress with an amendment giving women the right to vote. A senator agreed to formally introduce it to Congress, but it would not be until 1920 when it was finally ratified as the Nineteenth Amendment.

The Women's Rights Movement

On a hot summer day, July 13, 1848, five women gathered for tea in upstate New York. During their conversation, Elizabeth Cady Stanton asked why women were still not free in America's democracy, as they held no political power or voice in society. Her friends strongly agreed, and within two days they organized a convention to address the "social, civil, and religious condition and rights of women." This gathering became known as the Seneca Falls Convention, held on July 19–20, 1848.

Elizabeth wrote a Declaration of Sentiments and used the Declaration of Independence as her framework for thinking in her planning for the convention. She connected the budding Women's Rights Movement to that powerful symbol of American liberty in a brilliant way.

She carefully outlined areas of life where women were mistreated or unequal:

- Women were not allowed to vote and had to submit to laws created only by men.
- A married woman could not own property but had to pay property taxes.
- Husbands could take any money she earned or inherited.
- Husbands had license to "imprison" and "chastise" (beat) their wives.
- Women had no rights in divorce or child custody.
- Only a few occupations were open for women workers, and they got paid much less than men. For example, women could not be doctors or lawyers.
- Colleges and universities did not accept women students.
- Women could not participate in the affairs of churches.
- Women were dependent on men and robbed of their self-confidence.
- Minority Black women had it even worse than majority white women.

The first women's convention drew huge crowds and would lead to several more from 1850 until the start of the Civil War. Elizabeth Cady Stanton and other women—such as Susan B. Anthony, Lucy Stone, and Sojourner Truth—organized and lectured in this movement for forty years.

Finally, the right for women to vote became the central issue, as the ability to vote would allow women to make other reforms.

Ultimately, it took seventy-two years for the Women's Rights Movement to achieve their first goal. In 1919, the American Senate finally passed the Nineteenth Amendment to give women voting rights.

On August 26, 1920, American Women finally won full voting rights.

In the following the years, women's double burden of household and career responsibilities remained an issue.

President John F. Kennedy established the President's Commission on the Status of Women in December 1961. The publication of the Commission's report in 1963 resulted in two immediate policy changes: the federal government had to hire for career positions solely on the requirements of the position and not sex; and the 1963 Equal Pay Act was passed. Men and women had to be paid equally for the same work.

Other Leaders of the Civil and Women's Rights Movements

SOJOURNER TRUTH

Truth was born into slavery in New York. When New York began the process of abolishing slavery, her owner promised to free her but then reneged. She later escaped with her infant daughter but was forced to leave her other children behind.

When Truth learned that her five-year-old son had been illegally sold to a plantation in Alabama, she took the issue to the Supreme Court of New York. She was able to recover him and was the first Black woman to win such a case against a white man.

She spent most of her life fighting against slavery and for women's rights. She helped recruit Black troops during the Civil War. When she died, almost a thousand people attended her service.

HARRIET TUBMAN

Harriet Tubman was born into slavery in Maryland but later escaped to Philadelphia. She was part of thirteen missions that rescued about seventy slaves, including friends and family, using the Underground Railroad. During the Civil War, she served as a cook and nurse, then as a scout and spy for the Union. Later, she became an activist for the women's suffrage movement.

During the Civil War, she led a raid that liberated more than seven hundred slaves and is widely credited with being the first woman to lead an armed military operation in the U.S.

LUCY STONE

Along with Susan B. Anthony and Elizabeth Cady Stanton, Lucy Stone was part of a legendary "triumvirate" fighting for women's suffrage and feminism during the nineteenth century. She wrote extensively about women's rights, publishing speeches and writing many articles. She influenced Anthony to take up the cause, and Stanton wrote that Stone was the first person to stir the heart of the American public about women's rights.

Stone taught in district schools from the age of sixteen and was the first woman from Massachusetts to earn a college degree. She attended Oberlin College in Ohio, the first in the country to admit women and African Americans. To pay for school, she took up jobs teaching at district schools and housekeeping. But as she was paid much less than men for the same work, she had to work twice as many hours, which affected her health. When she asked the college for equal pay, she was refused. However, her students offered to pay if the college would not. After three months of pressure, the school relented and began equal pay for Stone and other women student teachers.

Stone spent decades in public service fighting for women's rights and helped make great strides in how society viewed women, marriage, and politics. When the women's movement itself split due to differences in ideology, it was Stone who, eighteen years later, brought the two sides back together and reunited them.

Stone gave her last public speeches at the World's Congress of Representative Women. Almost 500 women from 27 countries spoke, and 150,000 people attended. She died of cancer later that year. Well over a thousand people attended her funeral.

★ ★ ★ ★ ★

QUESTIONS 100-118: RECENT AMERICAN HISTORY AND OTHER IMPORTANT HISTORICAL INFORMATION

100. Name one war fought by the United States in the 1900s.*

- *World War I*
- *World War II*
- *Korean War*
- *Vietnam War*
- *(Persian) Gulf War*

First World War (1914-1918)

Also known as the Great War, the First World War started in July 1914 and lasted for four years until 1918. The U.S. entered the war in 1917, while Woodrow Wilson was president.

Historical strategists say that Europe had had a good balance of power before the First World War, but a crisis in the Balkan countries of Southeast Europe trigged a chain of events that shattered that balance. Slavic nationalists wanted to enlarge Serbia by annexing Bosnia, which was a province of Austria-Hungary.

On June 28, 1914, Archduke Franz Ferdinand of Austria was assassinated by Gavrilo Princip, and Austria-Hungary declared war on Serbia. This seemingly small conflict escalated rapidly. Soon, Russia, Germany, Great Britain, and France were all drawn into the war, primarily because they had signed treaties that obligated them to help defend others.

During the height of the war, the conflict was between Austria-Hungary, Bulgaria, Germany, and the Ottoman Empire on one side and Britain, France, Russia, Romania, Italy, Japan, and the U.S. (The Allied Powers) on the other side.

Historians say that competition among the countries, militarism, imperialism, the growth of nationalism, territorial disputes, and the arms races of previous decades all contributed to World War I.

In addition, misconceptions of intent (Germany thought Britain would remain neutral), fatalism about the inevitability of the war, and the speed at which the diplomatic crisis unfolded, combined to lead up to the war.

New military techniques and the horrors of trench warfare made World War I very costly. After the Allied Powers claimed victory, more than 10 million people were dead and 20 million were wounded.

At the Paris Peace Conference and Treaty of Versailles of 1919–20, various conditions were imposed on the defeated nations. Germany lost land and military, was forced to take official responsibility for the war, and was forced to pay war reparations that would be financially crippling to the national economy. The Russian, German, Austro-Hungarian, and Ottoman empires were dismantled. Borders changed, and new nations came into being including: Poland, Finland, the Baltic states, Czechoslovakia, and Yugoslavia.

The League of Nations was created, an attempt to bring all nations together to communicate and work together to avoid such wars in the future. However, the League was not strong enough to maintain peace. The pain and losses, as well as the many changes brought about by World War I, greatly unsettled Europe and directly led to the development of World War II.

Second World War (1939-1945)

There was much instability in Europe after the First World War. The German people felt humiliated and angry after the way they had been treated. With their economy struggling, they felt desperate. This made the people easy to manipulate when a charismatic leader came along and gave them a way to get their pride back.

Figure 12: © Shutterstock / zef art, used under license

Fascism and nationalism were also on the rise across Europe. Belief in German ethnic superiority would ultimately lead to genocide and the Holocaust, which would cause decades of pain and trauma.

In Asia, Japan had been rapidly industrializing for decades, making them suddenly much more powerful than other Asian nations. They eagerly adopted and purchased Western weapons and built up their military. Fascism and nationalism were also prevalent in

Japan. Believing in their ethnic superiority, they invaded China and Korea and sought to enslave all of Asia.

In Germany, the stage was set for Adolf Hitler, the leader of the Nazi Party, to form alliances with Italy and Japan. He wanted world domination and started by expanding the German empire, invading Poland in 1939, forcing Britain and France to declare war. The conflict in Europe quickly turned extremely bloody and went on far longer than anyone predicted.

In Asia, Japan was furious at U.S. sanctions and them aiding China. They desperately needed access to resources, including fuel, to continue their war. Furious at the Americans and unaware of the consequences of their actions, Japan attacked Pearl Harbor, which brought America into the war in Asia. They also attacked the Philippines, Guam, Wake Island, and the British Empire in Malaya, Singapore, and Hong Kong. America responded with force.

WAR CRIMES

Over the years, before and during the war, Nazi Germans conducted widespread genocide, slaughtering 6 million Jews, about two-thirds of the Jews in Europe. They also murdered about 5 million others including prisoners of war, Roma, people with disabilities, the mentally ill, homosexuals, Freemasons, and others, housing them in concentration or death camps until they could be exterminated. The Nazis forced about 12 million people to work in slave-like conditions throughout the economy. German soldiers raped as many as 10 million women in the Soviet Union alone.

The Imperial Japanese operated in much the same way as the Nazis. They enslaved millions of Chinese and Koreans, including forcing women into sexual slavery. When they invaded Nanjing, they raped and murdered up to three hundred thousand people. Estimates vary, with Japan causing somewhere between five million and thirty million civilian deaths.

Both the Nazi Germans and the Imperial Japanese conducted

biological experiments and chemical weapons tests on people. The Soviet Union was also guilty of crimes including massacring 22,000 Polish officers, imprisoning and executing hundreds of thousands of political prisoners, and soldiers committing mass rape of as many as 2 million German women.

U.S. ENTRY TO THE WAR

The U.S. attempted to remain militarily neutral in the beginning, offering supplies and support to Chinese and Western allies. The American public refused to become involved. After Japan attacked Pearl Harbor and declared war on the U.S., their German allies also declared war on the U.S. Only then did America become militarily involved on both fronts, two years into the conflict.

VICTORY AND DEFEAT

Nazi Germany could not maintain a war on multiple fronts forever, especially after the Americans entered the war, adding further pressure. German forces slowly weakened and collapsed. Germany signed an unconditional surrender on May 7, 1945, after Hitler's suicide on April 30, 1945, and the surrender took full effect on May 8, 1945.

The American Navy strangled Japan's economy and cut off its ability to supply their new overseas territory and troops. America, Britain, and China demanded Japan's unconditional surrender. Japan rejected the idea because they thought they could end the war without consequences. The U.S. then dropped two atomic bombs on Hiroshima and Nagasaki. This was a destructive power unlike anything humanity had ever seen, and both cities were instantly destroyed. Thousands died in the blast and from radiation. Japan finally agreed to surrender.

AFTERMATH

The Second World War was one of the most destructive wars in human history. Historians estimate that 27,000 people were killed per day during the six years the war lasted. WWII was the deadliest war in history. Seventy to eighty-five million people died, more than half of them noncombatants.

The U.S. emerged from the Second World War as a global superpower, together with Russia. Peace, technological advancements, rebuilding in other countries, and a baby boom caused the U.S. economy to soar. America's gross national product (G.N.P.), which measures all goods and services produced, shot up to $300 billion between 1940 and 1960, making the U.S. the wealthiest and most commanding nation in the world.

Korean War (1950-1953)

The Korean War was between North and South Korea, but also a proxy war between the U.S. on one side and China and the Soviet Union on the other. It was part of the Cold War.

In 1910, Japan invaded Korea and turned it into a slave state. In 1945, at the end of WWII and after a great deal of trauma, Korea was freed. At the time, Soviet forces were deployed in the northern half, and U.S. forces were deployed in the southern half.

Leaders in both the north and south declared themselves the sole ruler of Korea. Backed by the Soviets, North Korea attacked South Korea. The United Nations denounced the attack. Twenty-one countries, led by the U.S.A, tried to repel the invasion.

About 1 million soldiers and 2-3 million civilians died. Although fighting stopped when the two sides signed an armistice, no peace treaty was ever signed, so officially the war continues today, decades later. North and South continue to have strained relations.

North Korea has regularly threatened South Korea, Japan, and America. So many global sanctions have been placed against the country that they have been largely cut off from the rest of the world, except for support from Russia and China. Their economy revolves entirely around their military, and the population suffers under the totalitarian rule of the Kim Dynasty.

Vietnam War (1955-1975)

The Vietnam War was another proxy war, part of the Cold War between the U.S.A on one side and the Soviet Union and China on the other. North Vietnam was supported by the Soviets and China while South Vietnam was supported by the U.S.

Vietnam was formerly a French colony. It gained independence in 1954 but was divided into two parts. Guerilla warfare between the two sides increased over time, and as more and more soldiers entered combat, with steep losses, U.S. troop morale plummeted. Rape and civilian deaths were common. Drug use was rampant.

The U.S. government tried to keep the truth of the war from the American public, but in 1971, the Pentagon Papers were leaked to *The New York Times*, detailing these deceptions. Public sentiment became increasingly ugly against the war effort. Mass protests broke out.

During the war, the U.S. military made widespread use of chemicals to reduce the thick jungle that had been used so effectively to conduct guerilla warfare. Some 20% of the jungle and 20–36% of the mangrove forests were destroyed. Millions of people suffered from chemical poisoning and subsequent diseases and cancers.

For decades, the Vietnam War played a huge role in American culture and anti-war sentiments.

(Persian) Gulf War (1991)

In 1990, Iraq invaded Kuwait over oil and debt. This was immediately condemned by the UN. Multiple countries, led by the U.S., quickly responded.

With advancing technology, this was the first war covered live on television in real time and on the battlefield. It made Operation Desert Storm famous.

War in Iraq (Second Persian Gulf War) (2003-2011)

The War in Iraq in 2003 (also called the Second Persian Gulf War) consisted of two phases.

In the first phase, America said that Iraq had been illegally building weapons of mass destruction (nuclear). Action had to be taken because there was a danger to U.S. security. U.S. and British troops invaded and quickly defeated the Iraqi military.

In the second phase, the occupation of Iraq by U.S.-led allies was opposed by a rebellion. However, the violence eventually declined from 2007, and the U.S. started to withdraw from Iraq, completing the process in December 2011.

Investigations during and after the conflict showed that Iraq never had any weapons of mass destruction.

101. Why did the United States enter World War I?

- *Because Germany attacked U.S. (civilian) ships*
- *To support the Allied Powers (England, France, Italy, and Russia)*
- *To oppose the Central Powers (Germany, Austria-Hungary, the Ottoman Empire, and Bulgaria)*

102. When did all women get the right to vote?

- *1920*
- *After World War I*
- *(With the) 19th Amendment*

103. What was the Great Depression?

- *Longest economic recession in modern history*

104. When did the Great Depression start?

- *The Great Crash (1929)*
- *Stock market crash of 1929*

The Great Depression

The Great Depression was the most prolonged economic recession in modern history, and began during the summer of 1929. It became markedly worse in late 1929 and officially started when the stock markets crashed in October 1929. As a result, production and prices fell quickly. Bank and farm failures followed.

Figure 13: © Shutterstock / Everett Collection, used under license

At its lowest point in 1933, industrial production in the U.S. declined by more than 45%, and the G.D.P. fell 30%. The unemployment rate exceeded 20%. To know just how severe this was, one can compare it to America's next worst recession in 2007–2009.

Here, the G.D.P. declined only 4.3%, and the unemployment rate did not reach 10%.

Farm families migrated to California in search of a better life, and minority groups were worse off than usual. The Great Depression lasted for a decade until 1939, after which things slowly got better.

The U.S. president during most of the Great Depression was Franklin D. Roosevelt. He became president in 1933 and took immediate action to address America's economic woes. In his first one hundred days in office, his administration passed legislation to stabilize production, create jobs, and stimulate recovery.

America's entry into the Second World War after the Japanese attack on Pearl Harbor in late 1941 caused a surge in manufacturing, creating jobs and military enlistment and effectively ending the Great Depression.

105. Who was president during the Great Depression and World War II?

- *(Franklin) Roosevelt*

Franklin D. Roosevelt (FDR)

Roosevelt was president for four terms from 1933–1945, the longest-serving president and the only one to serve more than two terms.

Roosevelt was elected during the Great Depression and immediately brought about significant legislation to combat it, including major regulatory reforms in finance, communications, and labor. His most famous piece of legislation is the New Deal. This provided relief for the unemployed, insured bank deposits, established the Securities and Exchange Commission, and raised rural incomes. Roosevelt's reforms helped many people find work and stabilized the economy.

Roosevelt's legislation encouraged the construction of public works, libraries, parks, environmental conservation, and more. He invested in the arts, guaranteed workers the right to unionize, introduced pension and benefits with the Social Security Act, prohibited child labor, created the 40-hour work week, and created the minimum wage.

Roosevelt was a heavy smoker and suffered from multiple health complications, leading to his death in office in 1945. He is considered one of the most important people in U.S. history and one of the top three presidents.

106. Why did the United States enter World War II?

- *(Bombing of) Pearl Harbor*
- *Japanese attacked Pearl Harbor*
- *To support the Allied Powers (England, France, and Russia)*
- *To oppose the Axis Powers (Germany, Italy, and Japan)*

The Axis powers of WWII were Nazi Germany, Fascist Italy, and Imperial Japan. All three were highly expansionist, aggressive, nationalistic, and believed their people were superior to everyone else.

The Axis powers were defeated by the Allies, led by Britain, the U.S.A., and the Soviet Union.

107. Dwight Eisenhower is famous for many things. Name one.

- *General during World War II*
- *President at the end of (during) the Korean War*
- *34th president of the United States*
- *Signed the Federal-Aid Highway Act of 1956 (Created the Interstate System)*

Dwight D. Eisenhower

Dwight D. Eisenhower was a soldier graduating from West Point in 1915. He applied to serve in World War I but was denied. He served in the U.S. and the Philippines until World War II, rising to brigadier general.

When the U.S. entered World War II, Eisenhower oversaw the Allied invasions of Africa and Sicily, then France and Germany, as the Supreme Commander of the Allied Expeditionary Force.

After the war, he served as military governor of occupied Germany, Army Chief of Staff, president of Columbia University, and as the first supreme commander of N.A.T.O.

In 1952, Eisenhower became the thirty-fourth president of the U.S., serving from 1953–1961. He strove to contain communism and reduce the federal deficit. He led the creation of NASA (then called NACA), promoted science-based education, and pursued the space race. He was against spending too much on the military and the military-industrial complex.

108. Who was the United States' main rival during the Cold War?

- *Soviet Union*
- *USSR*
- *Russia*

109. During the Cold War, what was <u>one</u> main concern of the United States?

- *Communism*
- *Nuclear war*

The Cold War (1947-1991)

America and Russia (the U.S.SR) had been allies during the Second World War. However, the two former allies began to build up their own influence zones and divided the world into opposing camps. The main concern for America and its allies in the Western world was Russian communism.

The two adversaries never fought directly, because this could have easily led to a nuclear war. A massive stockpile of weaponry on both sides deterred the other side from directly attacking.

The two superpowers fought indirectly in proxy wars, the space race, and an arms race between 1945 and 1991. Examples of proxy wars include the Korean War and the Vietnam War. The United States entered these wars to stop the spread of communism.

The Cold War ended with the fall of the Berlin Wall in 1989 and when communist regimes collapsed in Eastern Europe shortly thereafter.

110. Why did the United States enter the Korean War?

- *To stop the spread of communism*

111. Why did the United States enter the Vietnam War?

- *To stop the spread of communism*

112. What did the Civil Rights Movement do?

- *Fought to end racial discrimination*

113. Martin Luther King, Jr. is famous for many things. Name one. *

- *Fought for civil rights*
- *Worked for equality for all Americans*
- *Worked to ensure that people would "not be judged by the color of their skin, but by the content of their character"*

The Civil Rights Movement

After the Civil War, slavery in America largely came to an end. However, discrimination against black people did not stop. Racism was still rampant, especially in the American South.

The Civil Rights Movement started as a struggle for social justice. The movement fought to end racial discrimination. Black Americans had had enough of prejudice and violence and fought for equal rights under American law. In the end, the movement spanned more than two decades.

Martin Luther King Jr. was a famous civil rights activist. He worked to get equality for all Americans. He said that, "People should not be judged by the color of their skin, but rather by the content of their character."

Eventually, the Civil Rights Act of 1964 outlawed segregation in jobs, schools, and public places. The Voting Rights Act of 1965 stated that anyone could vote, and the Fair Housing Act (1968) gave Black Americans the right to live where they wanted to.

However, despite these laws, Americans are still not entirely equal today. There has been significant progress over the years, but various Americans remain socially disadvantaged.

Martin Luther King Jr.

"I have a dream."

Martin Luther King Jr. was an American pastor, humanitarian, activist, and leader in the African American Civil Rights Movement. He did not use violence. He chose to use a pacifist type of civil disobedience to achieve his social change goals.

King said that all races should be treated equally, and he gave speeches to encourage African Americans not to use violence but rather to protest peacefully. Peaceful strategies included boycotts, sit-ins, and protest marches. King was one of the great speakers of modern times, and his speeches still inspire people today.

Martin Luther King Jr. helped organize a 1963 march in Washington, where he delivered his "I Have a Dream" speech. As a result, he won the Nobel Peace Prize in 1964.

Figure 14: © Shutterstock / FStreet, used under license

His successes, unfortunately, also made him a target of conservative people who feared change. As a result, King was arrested over twenty times, and his home was bombed. King was assassinated on April 4, 1968 on the balcony of a motel in Memphis.

114. Why did the United States enter the Persian Gulf War?

- *To force the Iraqi military from Kuwait*

115. What major event happened on September 11, 2001 in the United States? *

- *Terrorists attacked the United States*
- *Terrorists took over two planes and crashed them into the World Trade Center in New York City*
- *Terrorists took over a plane and crashed into the Pentagon in Arlington, Virginia*
- *Terrorists took over a plane originally aimed at Washington, D.C., and crashed in a field in Pennsylvania*

September 11, 2001

On this day, called 9/11, suicide bombers hijacked four airliners and carried out attacks against targets in the United States. Two planes were flown into the World Trade Center towers in New York while a third hit the Pentagon. The last plane crashed into a Pennsylvania field. Almost 3,000 people were killed on this tragic day. An extremist group called Al-Qaeda, and its leader, Osama bin Laden, took responsibility for the attacks. The alleged motivation for the attack was a holy war against the U.S. in retaliation for atrocities against Muslims.

116. Name one U.S. military conflict after the September 11, 2001 attacks.

- *(Global) War on Terror*
- *War in Afghanistan*
- *War in Iraq*

After September 11, 2001

These lethal terrorist attacks led to far-reaching changes in the anti-terror approach of the United States and around the world.

The U.S. government launched an ongoing military campaign called the Global War on Terror in response to 9/11. It was intended to be a new phase in global politics and affected international law, human rights, cooperation, governance, and security. The U.S. also sought to punish those behind the 9/11 attacks, particularly the leader, Osama bin Laden. They found him in Afghanistan.

The Taliban in Afghanistan refused to turn Osama bin Laden over to the U.S., leading the U.S. to declare war. During the war in Afghanistan, American warplanes bombed Taliban targets and bases belonging to Al-Qaida. An estimated 240,000 people died as a direct result of the invasion of Afghanistan meant to topple the Taliban. At least 2.7 million Afghan people had to flee because of the war, becoming refugees in Pakistan, Iran, and beyond.

The war in Afghanistan continued even after Osama bin Laden was located and killed in 2011 during a U.S. special operations mission in Pakistan. His death marked a significant moment in the conflict, but did not end it. The United States remained in Afghanistan to prevent the Taliban from regaining control and to support the development of a new, democratic government. Over time, U.S. forces were gradually reduced as the situation appeared to stabilize, although challenges on the ground persisted.

On August 15, 2021, with occupying forces reduced, the Taliban retook Kabul, and the Afghanistan government collapsed. The U.S.

decided to continue to support Afghanistan through diplomacy, humanitarian aid, and refugee programs instead of military involvement. On August 30, America's longest war to date officially ended when the last of the U.S. troops were finally transported out of Kabul.

117. Name one American Indian tribe in the United States.

- *Apache*
- *Blackfeet*
- *Cayuga*
- *Cherokee*
- *Cheyenne*
- *Chippewa*
- *Choctaw*
- *Creek*
- *Crow*
- *Hopi*
- *Huron*
- *Inupiat*
- *Lakota*
- *Mohawk*
- *Mohegan*
- *Navajo*
- *Oneida*
- *Onondaga*
- *Pueblo*
- *Seminole*
- *Seneca*
- *Shawnee*

- *Sioux*
- *Teton*
- *Tuscarora*

For a complete list of tribes, please visit: https://www.bia.gov/.

The First Peoples in the Americas

The exact nature of how people first came to the Americas remains partially theoretical because it happened so long ago, and evidence is limited, though it includes both D.N.A. and archeological records.

The most commonly accepted theory is that they first arrived approximately 26,000 to 19,000 years ago, when the waters between Siberia and Alaska were frozen. This allowed people to migrate across the Beringia land bridge. They were likely following and hunting herds of mammoth or other animals. On foot or by boat, they eventually moved down into North and South America, starting along the Pacific Coast and moving inland. This process took thousands of years.

Over time, people multiplied as they spread out, forming many different tribes. Some tribes remained hunter-gatherers for thousands of years while others settled and farmed both land and sea. They built towns and cities, just like other humans were doing elsewhere on the planet.

They became very established. Before the Europeans arrived, the population of all the Americas (North, Central, and South) was estimated at 50–100 million people. The population of Tenochtitlan, now Mexico City, once had a population of 200,000 people, comparable to the largest cities in Europe at the time.

However, before the arrival of Columbus, the peoples of the Americas were physically cut off from Europe and Asia. Advancements in art, writing, mathematics, science, and technology evolved and spread in other parts of the world, but they could not reach the Americas. This led to a significant difference in levels of organization, technology, and weapons. While isolated, peoples in the Americas were not exposed to diseases from other continents and were unable to build immunity to them, so they remained vulnerable.

These differences would lead to their decline following large-scale European arrivals. Sometimes, European and American cultures met and cooperated in peace. However, meetings more often resulted in war and other conflicts as Europeans tried to dominate the continent.

That clash of peoples and cultures is a defining part of American history. While conflict continues today in various forms, the descendants of Indigenous Americans are an important and an often-proud part of American society.

Conflict with Indigenous Peoples

Human societies are constantly in motion. We frequently compete over land and control, and this has often led to war. When the Europeans arrived in the Americas, they were more technologically advanced, more organized, and the Indigenous population increasingly dwindled due to new diseases brought over by explorers and conquerors.

Indigenous people were captured as slaves, died in military conquest, and were abused in many different ways. Those who survived became discriminated against socially, legally, and politically in ways still felt today.

However, Native Americans, like other groups, have benefitted from social and legal improvements aimed at promoting acceptance and equality. When the Europeans first arrived, there were 4-18 million Indigenous Americans in what is now the U.S.A. By 1890, that number had dropped to a mere 270,000. However, during the Twenty-First century, the population has increased, with over 3.7 million people identifying as American Indians, and another 5.9 million identifying as having mixed ancestry.

Valued Contributions from American Indians to Modern America

The various American Indian tribes have made significant contributions to modern society.

The potato, tomato, corn, chocolate, and coca, some of the world's most eaten foods, originated in the Americas and were farmed by several Indigenous groups.

Many medicines 'discovered' by Europeans in the Americas were actually made when Indigenous peoples shared their knowledge of the medicinal properties of local plants.

While cooking over fire is an ancient practice, the process of modern barbecuing comes from the Arawak people of the Caribbean and the Timucua people of Florida. When Columbus arrived in 1492, they found the Taino people roasting meat in the same way we do today.

Rubber was first used by Indigenous peoples in the Americas to make sports balls, containers, textile waterproofing, and more. The kayak, a narrow watercraft with a double-bladed paddle, was developed by the Inuit people in the Arctic. The Inuit also invented snow goggles. Other Indigenous inventions from the Americas include cable suspension bridges (originally made from grass by the Incas), raised-bed agriculture, baby bottles, syringes, hammocks, oral contraceptives, and mouthwash.

Of incredible importance is the Iroquois Confederacy. This style of governing was a model used by many Founding Fathers when designing the early United States governance structure. They sought a way to diversify power between states while also uniting them in order to create a framework of government that was much more democratic than the monarchies of Europe, which many new Americans hated. When seeking to create their ideal nation, they used the Indigenous peoples as inspiration.

The leader of the Onondaga tribe was called Canassatego. He urged the American colonies to unite and share the Iroquois Great

Law of Peace. Benjamin Franklin shared Canassatego's words with his fellow colonists and invited the Iroquois Grand Council of Chiefs to speak to the Continental Congress in 1776. The Indigenous people's example led to the principle of checks and balances between branches of power in government, the impeachment process, and more.

North American Natives have often appeared in literature, TV, film, and music. Many place names come from Indigenous people's names or words. Things such as the tomahawk, feather headdress, and totem pole have become symbols of American Indigenous peoples recognized all over the world.

Famous and Influential Indigenous Americans

POCAHONTAS (C.1595-C.1617)

In May 1607, the first English settlers arrived in what would later become the U.S.A. They founded the Jamestown colony. When members of the Powhaten tribal nation kidnapped a member of the colony, John Smith, and prepared to kill him, the daughter of the Powhaten leader, Pocahontas, intervened to save his life. She became an emissary to his people, leading to an attempt to coexist. However, as the colony desperately struggled to survive, relations between the colonists and the Powhaten fell apart. The two sides went to war. Pocahontas was told that John Smith was killed, though he actually returned to England.

Later, Pocahontas met and married colonist John Rolfe in 1614, a union blessed by both cultures. It led to peace. Pocahontas, her son with Rolfe, and some of her people were taken to England, and she became an important cultural symbol for those wanting to prove colonization of America was possible. In London, she was given the name Rebecca and displayed like a princess. She attended social events and even met the royal family. She had a portrait done of her, the only image ever drawn of her in person.

At age twenty or twenty-one, Pocahontas attempted to return

home to America in 1617, but she suddenly became gravely ill and died. Many believe it was from an illness such as tuberculosis, pneumonia, dysentery, or smallpox, but some believe she was poisoned. She was buried in Gravesend, England.

John Rolfe returned to America but left his son, Thomas, in England with relatives. However, Thomas returned to America twenty years later to become a successful farmer. Their descendants continue to live in America today.

Pocahontas and her life story have been highly romanticized in literature, film, and song. She is perhaps the most famous of all Native Americans.

Pocahontas is actually a nickname, which means "little mischief." Her real name was Matoax, though this was kept hidden out of superstition until after her marriage.

GERONIMO (1829-1909)

During his own time, Geronimo was a very famous leader and a medicine man of the Apache tribe. He refused to allow the U.S. government to confine his people on reservations and repeatedly broke out with his warriors in attempts to fight back and free his people. He went to war with Mexico when their soldiers murdered his wife, children, and mother. He devoted his entire life to resisting U.S. encroachment, avenging his murdered family, and fighting for his people to have a home.

He was the last Indigenous leader to surrender to the U.S. military. The final twenty years of his life were spent as a prisoner and a tourist attraction. He was frequently displayed at fairs and exhibitions in old west shows, and even in a parade to prove how the

U.S. military was victorious over the Native American tribes, showing that the 'savage' responsible for killing so many Americans had been 'tamed'.

Tourists would approach him and ask for mementos. Geronimo would cut buttons off his shirt and sell them for twenty-five cents. Then, he would buy more buttons, sew them on, and sell more. He did the same with his hats. He was forced to pose for photographs and make crafts to sell.

This treatment made him widely famous. It was intended to portray him and his people as weak and defeated. However, his name came to be associated with great bravery, his story made known to all and preserved for generations. His fierce resistance and determination very much epitomized the rebellious spirit that the American people have always been proud of.

QUEEN LILI'UOKALANI (1837-1917)

Lili'uokalani was the first woman to rule Hawaii, and the region's last Indigenous leader during a time when European and American governments were trying to take control of the archipelago. Wealthy sugar and pineapple barons held a great deal of power, and some were keen to force Hawaii to become part of the U.S.A.

During her first regency, she adeptly handled a very dangerous smallpox epidemic that killed over a third of the Hawaiians infected. She set aside land for a leprosy hospital at Kaka'ako. She founded a bank for women and founded an educational society for girls.

During her reign, she fought to maintain Hawaiian sovereignty and create a new constitution to strengthen the Hawaiian monarchy and resist foreign influence. The new constitution would have restored voting rights to poor native Hawaiians and Asians.

Anti-monarchists, reformers, and those striving to have Hawaii annexed by the U.S.A fought against the queen. Many of these people were American and European citizens living in Hawaii, and most

Figure 15: © Shutterstock / Everett Collection, used under license were driven by personal political and business interests, uncaring of the welfare of the native Hawaiians. They staged an illegal coup and deposed the queen.

Lili'uokalani officially relinquished power to the U.S.A., hoping they would support her and restore the monarchy. However, those behind the coup immediately travelled to Washington D.C. to petition for annexation. President Cleveland's administration investigated the coup and declared it illegal. He offered to restore Lili'uokalani to the throne if she granted amnesty to those who had overthrown her. She responded by saying Hawaiian law called for confiscating the property of the criminals and the death penalty for treason. Although these laws were similar to American laws, President Cleveland withdrew his personal support and sent the issue to Congress. Congress absolved those behind the coup of all responsibility and allowed them to maintain control.

When a peaceful solution, much patience, and diplomacy failed, supporters rebelled to try and restore the queen and the monarchy. The rebellion was put down, and the former queen was arrested and sentenced to five years of hard labor. The illegal government threatened to execute all her supporters, unless she officially abdicated the throne.

> *For myself, I would have chosen death rather than to have signed it; but it was represented to me that by my signing this paper all the persons who had been arrested, all my people now in trouble by reason of their love and loyalty towards me, would be immediately released. Think of my position—sick, a lone woman in prison, scarcely knowing who was my friend, or who listened to my words only to betray me, without legal advice or friendly counsel, and the stream of blood ready to flow unless it was stayed by my pen.*

—Queen Lili'uokalani, *Hawaii's Story by Hawaii's Queen*

Two years later, despite very strong opposition from Hawaiians, the U.S. officially annexed Hawaii. Upon Lili'uokalani's death, her estate was donated to a trust that cared for orphans and poor children.

Queen Lili'uokalani was a skilled musical composer and created the Hawaiian national anthem, "Aloha Oe." She could play the guitar, piano, organ, ukulele, and zither, as well as sing. Lili'uokalani was esteemed around the world during her own time, beloved by many of her people, and continues to be a deeply revered figure in Hawaii today.

118. Name one example of an American innovation.

- *Light bulb*
- *Automobile (cars, internal combustion engine)*
- *Skyscrapers*
- *Airplane*
- *Assembly line*
- *Landing on the moon*
- *Integrated circuit (IC)*

★ ★ ★ ★ ★

QUESTIONS 119-128:
SYMBOLS AND HOLIDAYS

A. Symbols

119. What is the capital of the United States?

- *Washington, D.C.*

120. Where is the Statue of Liberty?

- *New York (Harbor)*
- *Liberty Island [Also acceptable are New Jersey, near New York City, and on the Hudson (River).]*

121. Why does the flag have 13 stripes? *

- *Because there were) 13 original colonies*
- *(Because the stripes) represent the original colonies)*

The American Flag

Figure 16: © Shutterstock / Buch and Bee, used under license

Flags identify a nation whose people share the same values and follow the same set of rules and regulations. The American flag has played a role in both nationalism and rebellion and is an essential part of American history.

Also referred to as the Stars and Stripes, The Star-Spangled Banner, or Old Glory, the American flag symbolizes freedom and liberty. The use of the color red represents courage. Blue represents vigilance, perseverance, and justice. White symbolizes purity.

There have been twenty-seven official versions of the flag, with each new flag reflecting the addition of more states over the years. The first flag had thirteen stars (for the thirteen states) and thirteen stripes (for the thirteen original colonies). Over time, the number of states increased, and stars were added, resulting in the flag now consisting of thirteen stripes representing the thirteen original colonies and fifty stars representing each state in America.

The current version of the American flag was designed as part of a class project by a seventeen-year-old scholar named Robert G. Heft in 1949. It was later accepted and approved by President Eisenhower as the national flag of the U.S.A.

The American flag is a representation of honor, pride, and liberty. It is common practice for war veterans and government officials to have the flag draped over their coffins. Afterward, the flag gets folded into a triangle, representing the hat of General George Washington while at the same time paying tribute to all those who have lost their lives while in military service.

122. Why does the flag have 50 stars?

- *(Because there is) one star for each state*
- *(Because) each star represents a state*
- *(Because there are) 50 states*

States

The United States is a federal republic composed of fifty states: Alabama, Alaska, Arizona, Arkansas, California, Colorado, Connecticut, Delaware, Florida, Georgia, Hawaii, Idaho, Illinois, Indiana, Iowa, Kansas, Kentucky, Louisiana, Maine, Maryland, Massachusetts, Michigan, Minnesota, Mississippi, Missouri, Montana, Nebraska, Nevada, New Hampshire, New Jersey, New Mexico, New York, North Carolina, North Dakota, Ohio, Oklahoma, Oregon, Pennsylvania, Rhode Island, South Carolina, South Dakota, Tennessee, Texas, Utah, Vermont, Virginia, Washington, West Virginia, Wisconsin, and Wyoming.

A star on the star-spangled banner represents each one of these states. That is why you will find fifty stars on the American flag.

Territories

The United States has various territories: Puerto Rico, American Samoa, Guam, the Northern Mariana Islands, and the U.S. Virgin Islands. Each territory has a distinct history and culture and governs itself under the authority of the U.S. government. They are located in the Caribbean and the South Pacific Ocean.

In the past, territories have been helpful to the U.S. because of their natural resources or because they were military outposts.

A territory can be incorporated, which means that the U.S. Constitution applies there. However, it can also be unincorporated, with the Constitution only partially applying. The only incorporated territory is Palmyra Atoll, owned by the U.S. Nature Conservancy and the U.S. Fish and Wildlife Service. It houses only scientists and researchers.

Most territories are organized, meaning they can manage their affairs under their own governments. The only unorganized territory is American Samoa. It has no government and is regulated by an organic act.

American territories are not states and do not have full recognition. However, territories can send a delegate to the House of Representatives. Except for the American Samoa people, the other four territories' residents are U.S. citizens. They can vote in the primary elections for president but not in general elections.

123. What is the name of the national anthem?

- *The Star-Spangled Banner*

The National Anthem

Francis Scott Key watched American soldiers raise the American flag over Fort McHenry in Baltimore, Maryland in 1814. It touched a chord, and he wrote a poem that was eventually accepted as the National Anthem of America in 1931. Congress made a resolution in this regard, signed by President Herbert Hoover.

Today, you can hear the patriotic tune, "The Star-Spangled Banner," at sporting events, carnivals, parades, and political gatherings throughout America.

124. The Nation's first motto was "E Pluribus Unum." What does that mean?

- *Out of many, one*
- *We all become one*

B. Holidays

125. What is Independence Day?

- *A holiday to celebrate U.S. independence (from Britain)*
- *The country's birthday*

126. Name three national U.S. holidays. *

- *New Year's Day*
- *Martin Luther King, Jr. Day*
- *Presidents Day (Washington's Birthday)*
- *Memorial Day*
- *Independence Day*
- *Labor Day*
- *Columbus Day*
- *Veterans Day*
- *Thanksgiving Day*
- *Christmas Day*

New Year's Day

January 1 each year is a joyous occasion. The celebrations start at midnight with fireworks exploding and people drinking champagne.

Martin Luther King Jr. Day

Every third Monday of January, Americans celebrate Martin Luther King Jr., the prominent American Civil Rights Movement leader. He was a firm believer in equality for all and non-violent activism.

This day is usually celebrated with parades and speeches made by political leaders.

Presidents' Day (George Washington's Birthday)

There is a celebration for all presidents on the third Monday in February. Initially, this day was intended to celebrate the birth and life of George Washington, who was born on February 22, 1732, the first-ever president of the United States of America.

Memorial Day

Memorial Day honors the men and women who have died serving America in the military. People wear red poppy flowers and come to a quiet standstill at 3:00 p.m. The holiday is celebrated on the last Monday in May. It is also a long weekend for many Americans to enjoy with family and friends, as it is the unofficial start of summer.

Juneteenth

June 19 is a federal holiday commemorating the end of slavery. The date comes from 1865 when the final enforcement of the Emancipation Proclamation happened in Texas during the Civil War. Some of the first celebrations date back to 1866 and it became an official holiday in 2021.

Independence Day

July 4 marks Independence Day. It is often called The Fourth of July and celebrates the original Declaration of Independence in 1776. This day is celebrated with fireworks, parades, carnivals, family barbeques, and picnics. The American Flag is often prominent.

Labor Day

Labor Day is a celebration of American workers' social and economic achievements. It takes place on the first Monday in September. It is celebrated with parades, parties, picnics, and festivals and is also the unofficial last weekend of summer in the United States.

Columbus Day

On the second Monday in October each year, Americans commemorate Columbus's voyage to the New World. They honor the courage and determination, which enabled many to find freedom and opportunity in America.

In recent years, there has been a movement to replace Columbus Day with Indigenous Peoples' Day, and many states in America now observe the new commemoration. The first state to rename Columbus Day was South Dakota in 1990, and since then, many others have followed.

Veterans Day

Veterans Day celebrates the bravery and sacrifice of all the living U.S. veterans. It is not to be confused with Memorial Day. It is held on November 11 each year.

Thanksgiving

Thanksgiving is held on the fourth Thursday in November, celebrating the harvest and other blessings of the year. Families gather around a feast, which often includes turkey, cranberries, and pumpkin pie.

Christmas (December 25)

Christmas Day is celebrated by people worldwide, no matter their spiritual beliefs. It is a time to gather with family and friends, and it is traditional to exchange gifts. Common features include Christmas trees, Santa Claus, drinking eggnog, and building snowmen.

127. What is Memorial Day?

- *A holiday to honor soldiers who died in military service*

128. What is Veterans Day?

- *A holiday to honor people in the (U.S.) military*
- *A holiday to honor people who have served (in the U.S. military)*

★ ★ ★ ★ ★

A DETAILED LOOK AT THE U.S. CONSTITUTION

The Seven Articles of the Constitution

Overview

The articles of the Constitution explain the organization of the three political branches and how they interact with states. They explain how the Constitution can be amended, if necessary.

The first three articles of the U.S. Constitution establish the three branches of the government and outline the specific powers of each. Although power is separated, it is also shared in the sense that the actions of each branch can be checked by another and balanced if needed.

The legislative branch of government creates the laws of the land, but the president (part of the executive branch) may veto a law if two-thirds of Congress agrees. Any law can be found unconstitutional in a U.S. court of law, demonstrating the check and balance function of the judicial branch of the U.S. government.

- Article I of the U.S. Constitution deals with the legislative branch, the branch that can make laws. The article splits legislative powers into two chambers: the Senate and the House of Representatives. The article describes the organization of Congress and what specific powers it has, and what it is not allowed to do.
- Article II tackles the executive branch. The executive branch manages the day-to-day operations of the U.S. government through its various federal agencies and departments. The article describes how the president and the vice president should be elected, qualifications needed for office, and procedures to follow if the president should become unable to serve. It describes the powers of the president.
- Article III outlines the judicial branch. It brings the Supreme Court into being and allows Congress to establish lower federal courts. It states different cases and says which court can preside over them. Judges on the bench are assigned for life and can only be removed due to bad behavior.
- Article IV defines the relationship between the different states and the federal government. The federal government gives each state a republican form of government and oversees the people of each state. It says all states are equal (and so are their citizens) and that they should respect and honor each other's laws. A practical example is that driver's licenses issued by different states must be accepted across the United States of America.
- Article V states that future generations can amend the

Constitution if needed. An individual state or Congress can initiate the amendment process.

- Article VI is known as the supremacy clause. It determines that the U.S. Constitution is the "highest, the supreme law of the land," and all officials must swear an oath to the Constitution.
- Article VII is about ratification. It details all the people who signed the Constitution initially when there were just thirteen states.

Article I of the U.S. Constitution

Separating Powers

People need laws to govern behavior. Rulers have long realized that guidelines are the backbone of successful government. The Founding Fathers realized it, too. They knew that the legislature must be assertive, but not too powerful.

That is why the three main branches of government (legislative, executive, and judicial) have separate powers. They prevent one component from becoming tyrannical.

Two Houses

Legislative power is divided between two houses. This is called a bicameral legislature.

The first house is the House of Representatives, elected directly by the people. The House of Representatives has Representatives from each state based on its population. The second house is the Senate, comprised of Senators selected by state legislatures. In the Senate, two Senators for each state are allowed.

Congress (as these two houses became known under the U.S. Constitution) has an array of powers. It regulates internal and external trade, maintains diplomacy with other countries, taxes its people, maintains an army, declares war, coins money, and more. It also checks and balances the other two federal branches.

Article I Sections

Article I of the U.S. Constitution has ten different sections. Each section is broken down even further into different clauses.

SECTION 1

> *All legislative Powers herein granted shall be vested in a Congress of the United States, which shall consist of a Senate and House of Representatives.*

This vesting clause states that the newly formed Congress will have all the power to make laws for the country through a two-part body. The first of the three branches of government, the legislative branch, is established by Article I.

Articles II and III have similar vesting clauses, which give them their powers. In short, it means that no other branch of government has the same sort of power as the legislative branch.

SECTION 2

The second section of Article I gives us information about the first of the two legislative branches in the U.S. Congress, the U.S. House of Representatives.

Members will be elected every second year by the people of each state or district. You must be a U.S. citizen and at least twenty-five years old to be considered. A representative must have been an American citizen for at least seven years and live in the state you want to represent.

In the drafting of the U.S. Constitution, the drafters thought they could calculate the number of Representatives by using each state's total population. But who counts as a citizen? At that time, the south of America had lots of slaves, and some people wanted slaves to count. Luckily, after the Civil War, the issue became moot when slavery was abolished. After that, each person was counted equally.

Some states today have more Representatives than others because of the state's population. Over time, the American population has grown to such an extent that the total number of Representatives had to be capped. Today, it stands at 435. U.S. representatives serve shorter terms than U.S. senators so that public opinion can be more closely followed.

SECTION 3

Section 3 of Article I describes the working of the Senate. You must be at least thirty-years old to be a Senator, and they serve in six-year blocks.

There are two senators for each state appointed, for a total of 100 senators. The reason for this is equal representation for all states, even the smaller ones. To qualify, you must live in the appointed state and be a U.S. citizen for at least nine years.

The vice president is the leader of the Senate but is not allowed to vote unless they cannot decide because of a tie.

At first, at the drafting of the Constitution, it was decided that state legislatures would elect the Senate. This was because states did not want to lose their independence to a new federal government. By designing the election of senators this way, the Senate could be more responsive to state governments. As a result, state interests would not be lost in the higher federal government. This was only amended in 1913 when the people could directly elect their senators.

Section 3 gives instructions as to what would happen if a senator or government official violates the Constitution or commits a crime serious enough to warrant removal from office. This has been tested many times, starting with Andrew Johnson in 1868.

SECTION 4

This section explains that each state may decide how it will elect its members of Congress. It also says that Congress must meet at least once every year.

Initially, the states had free rein in deciding how to craft election rules. Today, states still regulate elections, but the Reconstruction Amendments to the Constitution (Amendments Thirteen to Fifteen) allow Congress to become more involved. Initially, the main issue was the integration of newly emancipated slaves into American politics. These three amendments give Constitutional civil and legal protections to former slaves.

In 1933, Amendment Twenty changed the date of the yearly Congressional meeting. Instead of it being on the first Monday in December, the meeting must take place by the third Monday in January. This amendment also changed the date of presidential inaugurations. Before, there had been more than a three-month gap between election and inauguration, but this amendment shortened the time. The president is now elected in November and sworn in in January instead of March.

SECTION 5

This section sets out essential procedures for Congress. It explains the qualifications of members, the quorum needed, the rules to follow, and how each House should keep a record. It also states that the two Houses cannot adjourn individually but must wait for each other to give permission.

While this section mainly lists rules, it also identifies an essential power of Congress: the ability to criticize those in power. In 1834, President Andrew Jackson was reprimanded for not revealing a document to Congress that he had already read to his advisors.

Attendance is another crucial topic in this section. Today's quorum for the House of Representatives is 218. For the Senate, it is fifty-one. The Constitution allows members of Congress to meet with other members in private (leaving the chamber) while still maintaining the quorum.

SECTION 6

What exactly may a Senator or a representative do and not do?

The members of Congress are paid, and they cannot be arrested, unless it is for a felony, treason, or disturbing of the peace. They cannot be detained when traveling to and from a Congress meeting. Members of Congress are not allowed to simultaneously hold any other office in the U.S. government.

The drafters of the original Constitution were against the abuses they had suffered in Great Britain from its monarchy, but some elements of the old English government stuck with them. For example, a clause in Section 6 states that a Congress member cannot be punished for giving an opinion. It is called the Speech or Debate Clause.

SECTION 7

Before a law is a law, it is called a bill. Senators or Representatives have ideas, called bills, that they think should become law. Bills start in the Senate or the House of Representatives. Section 7 of Article I explains the process. A bill can start in either one of the two Houses of Congress, but it must be passed in both Houses before it can become law.

If a senator takes a bill to fellow senators and they vote it down, the bill is dead. Should a majority agree that the bill should become law, it is passed over to the House of Representatives. They vote on the bill and discuss it. They can refer the bill back to the Senate for changes. If the Senate disagrees on changes, the bill is dead. Once the House and Senate both approve the bill, it is given to the president.

The president has the last say on each bill. When they sign it, it becomes law. They can also decide to veto the bill, in which case it will revert to Congress for a vote. If both Houses pass with a two-thirds majority vote, the veto can be overturned, and the bill will become law, regardless of what the president might want.

The original drafters of the Constitution were committed to creating a government for the people by the people, so the issue of taxation had to be as democratic as possible. They did this by stating that all laws about taxes must originate in the House of Representatives, as these were the people who would act in the interests of most of the citizens.

SECTION 8

The specific powers or duties of Congress (the House and the Senate) are set out in Section 8. The Founding Fathers wanted their new Congress to be democratic and fair, with no chance of oppressing the people.

Congress has the power to do the following:

- Tax citizens to provide for the general welfare and standard protection of the people as described in the Preamble. This includes the support of a military force, the building of roads, operating post offices, etc.
- Borrow money.
- Regulate commerce and business transactions by setting up standard rules for the conducting of business between different states, but also between other countries.
- Set Immigration and naturalization rules.
- Coin money and punish the counterfeiting of money.
- Establish post offices and a standardized mail system.
- Protect copyright, and therefore, its inventors and its authors.
- Establish federal courts below the Supreme Court
- Punish pirates. This was a pressing problem in the 1700s, as American ships were the target of pirates in the Mediterranean Sea.

- Declare war.
- Raise and support a military force. Before the Constitution, there was no national military.
- Control government areas.
- Create laws to fulfill the powers listed here. This power is also referred to as the Elastic Clause and allows rules to help execute the functions of Congress.

The powers listed here can be broken down into three areas: specific powers, implied powers, and inherent powers.

Specific powers, such as declaring war, were written down and clear in their intent.

Implied powers were general powers that were stated, but the Constitution does not go into detail. For instance, Clause 8 of Article 1 gives Congress the power to establish post offices and trusts that they will know what else is needed to let it all run smoothly.

Inherent powers are unlisted but are the powers that a government must have. A good example is the need to conduct foreign affairs. The Constitution does not discuss this in detail, but it still needs to be done because the United States is a country.

SECTION 9

There must be limits on Congress. This section states what Congress is not allowed to do and where they are prohibited from making laws.

Previously, the slave trade was protected to ensure the support of the southern states for the ratification of the Constitution. Today, this part of the Constitution is obsolete.

Section 9 gives citizens the privilege of the writ of habeas corpus. It means that no one can be jailed without reason, or held indefinitely without a trial. A public official must show a valid reason for the person's detention. There must be a lawful basis for detaining someone.

The Constitution prohibits the making and changing of laws in a way that could target certain people. For example, something might be currently legal, but a law is changed to make that activity suddenly illegal in a way that hurts an individual or group. This is called ex post facto law. Ex post facto means "after the fact," or from "after the action." It changes the legal consequences of actions that someone committed before the law went into effect. For example, an ex post facto law can make a crime worse by bringing it into a more severe category. Such laws are unconstitutional in the U.S. and are generally deemed unfair.

The section says that no title of nobility, such as king, queen, prince, or marquis, can ever be established.

SECTION 10

This section limits the powers of states. States cannot take on powers that were given to the federal government. By setting limits, the drafters of the Constitution ensured the supremacy of the national government.

For example, states cannot create money, declare war, tax goods from other states, or have their own navy. These powers are only for the federal government. States can, however, provide schooling and education, provide protection and safety, approve land use, and more.

Article II of the U.S. Constitution

The second Article of the U.S. Constitution outlines the executive branch's functions. It includes the Office of the President but also other executive officers, such as state governors, federal departments, agencies, and the Cabinet. In effect, the President oversees the executive branch.

The Founding Fathers realized that a leader was necessary, but that their powers had to be clearly defined. They did not want a tyrannical ruler like the King of England, so they decided on a president (and associated offices).

The president is the chief of the Army and the Navy. They can make treaties and appoint ambassadors, officials, and justices of the Supreme and federal courts. They can propose legislation, call Congress in for a special session, and report to them regularly.

The executive branch of the government administrates the day-to-day operations of each state and the country as a whole. Article II of the Constitution establishes how it is done.

The Organization of the Executive Branch and Cabinet

There are four divisions of the executive branch: the Cabinet, independent agencies, government corporations, and regulatory agencies.

The Constitution does not explicitly create the Cabinet. However, in 1789, President Washington felt he needed advisors. The Cabinet is a group of people who help the president with advice, and each oversees a department, of which there are fifteen in total. Cabinet members are called secretaries. Some of these departments are Agriculture, Treasury, Commerce, Defense, Education, Labor, Transportation, and more. Each secretary has many people working under them.

Independent Agencies are agencies, such as N.A.S.A. (National Aeronautics and Space Administration), the O.S.C. (Office of Special Counsel for federal whistleblowers), the S.B.A. (Small Business Administration), and the U.S.P.S. (United States Postal Service).

Government corporations are businesses run by the U.S. Government to provide services to American citizens. Examples include the U.S. Postal Service and the Federal Deposit Insurance Corporation (F.D.I.C.), which insures money deposited in banks.

Regulatory commissions ensure that large industries follow rules and that the public's safety is not jeopardized. Examples are the F.A.A. (Federal Aviation Administration), which regulates aircraft, pilots, and airports, and the F.C.C. (Federal Communications Commission), which licenses television and radio stations.

Article II Sections

SECTION 1

Section 1 describes the rights and roles of the President and the Vice President.

The first clause in this section is called the Vesting Clause, providing for an individual to take executive office: the president of the United States.

Alexander Hamilton, one of the framers of the Constitution, wanted to elect a single executive who could serve as president for life. However, many others believed this would be the same as a monarchy, and they rejected the idea. Together with the Vice president, the president shall be elected for a four-year term.

The Electoral College chooses the President and Vice President. Each state gets electors. A state's number of electors equals its U.S. representatives plus its two U.S. senators. Electors vote separately for president and vice president. A candidate must secure a majority of electoral votes to win. People who serve in the U.S. Congress, or who hold a federal office, cannot be electors.

In the early days of America, ordinary people were poorly educated and not informed. As a result, the electoral college was established to keep the people from making mistakes and choosing a terrible leader. Today, many people argue that voters are better informed and should determine their president directly. However, all attempts to change the way the president is elected have failed.

Should there not be a majority vote for a specific candidate, then the House of Representatives will vote, whereby each representative in the House has one vote. Two-thirds of the House must be represented in such voting for this to happen. The candidate who receives the second most votes will be appointed vice president.

Congress decides when and where presidential elections are to take place. It usually happens on the same date and simultaneously for all states.

For an individual to qualify as a presidential candidate, he or she must:

- Be a born U.S. citizen.
- Be at least thirty-five years of age.
- Be a resident in the U.S.A for fourteen years or longer.

If the president dies, resigns, or becomes unable to perform their duties, the vice president will take over. Should the vice president be unable to fulfill the role, another executive officer, such as the Speaker of the House, will step in until a suitable candidate has been elected.

The president's salary is determined by Congress and cannot change (either by increasing or decreasing) during their time in office. Currently, it is around $400,000 per year.

Before the president can officially begin their term and be sworn in as president, they must take an oath, which is called the oath of allegiance:

> *"I do promise that I will faithfully fulfill my role as President of the United States, and will preserve, protect, and defend the Constitution of the United States to the best of my abilities."*

"So help me God," is usually added by the president.

Both the President and the Vice President are elected just after the first Monday in November. Inauguration Day is January 20.

The executive branch must carry out the laws of the United States made by the legislative branch. The executive branch is enormous, and thousands of people work for the president.

SECTION 2

The president is the Commander in Chief. He or she is responsible for commanding the Army, Air Force, and the Navy. They may call upon the Cabinet to help in decision-making.

Furthermore, they are also able to grant pardons for federal crimes. (Governors and state pardon boards pardon state crimes.) The power of pardon means that the president may excuse someone for a crime they committed, giving them immunity.

According to the Advice and Consent Clause, the president may make treaties with foreign countries and appoint justices and government officials with the advice and approval of the Senate. Appointing judges is one of the checks the executive branch has over the judicial branch. The president may appoint individual offices while the Senate is in recess. These offices, however, will end as soon as the next Congress session starts.

SECTION 3

This section is about the responsibilities of the president.

The first clause of Section 3 of Article II is called the Recommendation Clause. Through the State of the Union address, the President must supply Congress with information about what is happening regarding the executive office, what he is doing, and plans he has in mind. The president may call a special session in times of crisis, although Congress may not be in session at that time. This may involve one or both houses.

The president's powers can be put into five categories: Commander in Chief, Chief of State, Chief Executive, Chief Legislator, and Chief of Party.

As Commander in Chief, the president is the highest military person in the U.S.. He is responsible for the navy, army, air force, and the marines.

As Chief of State, the president is tasked with receiving all foreign officials who come into America. He also represents the whole country when he travels to other countries to meet with other leaders.

As Chief Executive, the president must ensure that all his staff, cabinet, and other employees do their jobs correctly.

As Chief Legislator, the president can veto laws, and he is

empowered to make recommendations to Congress as he deems necessary. For example, he may recommend legislation and ask Congress to look at it and pass a particular bill.

As Chief of Party, the president is the head of his political party and makes decisions regarding the make-up of the party.

SECTION 4

This section determines that the president, vice president, or other government officials may be impeached (charged with committing a crime against the state) for treason, bribery, high crimes, or misdemeanors.

For the impeachment process to begin, the House of Representatives comes up with a list of charges against the official. The process continues in the Senate, where senators act as the jury and hear both sides of the case. If the president is being charged, the Chief Justice of the Supreme Court will be the judge. Eventually, two-thirds of the Senate must agree before the official can be convicted and removed from office.

In U.S. history, only three presidents have been impeached by the House of Representatives.

In 1867, President Andrew Johnson was charged with several offenses, but Johnson escaped being convicted with just one vote when the Senate held a trial.

In 1998, Bill Clinton was impeached because of perjury and obstruction of justice. However, the Senate found him not guilty, and he remained president until the end of 2001.

Donald Trump was the first president in the history of the United States to be impeached twice. The first charge was abuse of power and the obstruction of Congress in 2020. Trump was acquitted. In January 2021, Trump was again impeached for incitement of insurrection. It was after the disruption of a joint session of Congress to count electoral votes from the 2020 presidential election. The Senate voted, and Trump was again acquitted, 57–43.

None of these presidents or any other presidents in the history of the U.S.A, have ever been removed from office.

Article III of the U.S. Constitution

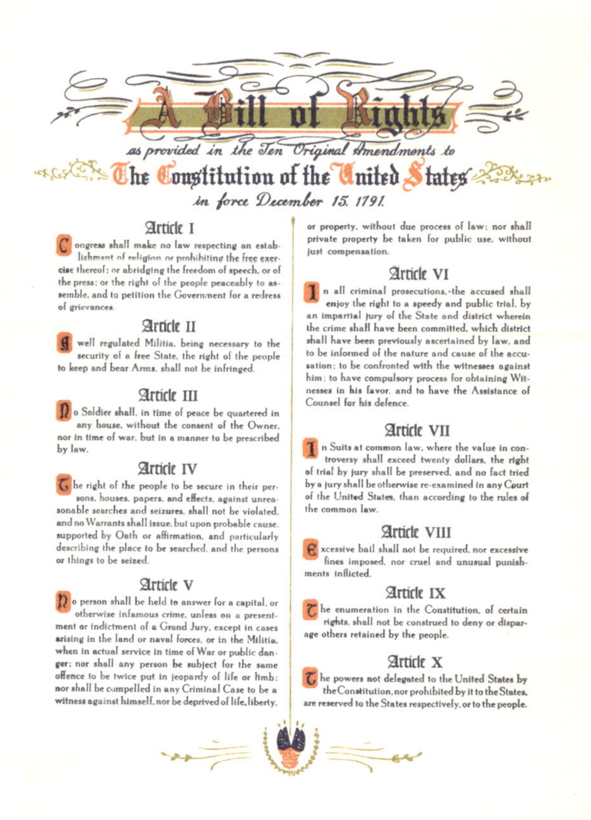

A Bill of Rights

as provided in the Ten Original Amendments to

The Constitution of the United States

in force December 15. 1791.

Article I

Congress shall make no law respecting an establishment of religion or prohibiting the free exercise thereof; or abridging the freedom of speech, or of the press; or the right of the people peaceably to assemble, and to petition the Government for a redress of grievances.

Article II

A well regulated Militia, being necessary to the security of a free State, the right of the people to keep and bear Arms, shall not be infringed.

Article III

No Soldier shall, in time of peace be quartered in any house, without the consent of the Owner, nor in time of war, but in a manner to be prescribed by law.

Article IV

The right of the people to be secure in their persons, houses, papers, and effects, against unreasonable searches and seizures, shall not be violated, and no Warrants shall issue, but upon probable cause, supported by Oath or affirmation, and particularly describing the place to be searched, and the persons or things to be seized.

Article V

No person shall be held to answer for a capital, or otherwise infamous crime, unless on a presentment or indictment of a Grand Jury, except in cases arising in the land or naval forces, or in the Militia, when in actual service in time of War or public danger; nor shall any person be subject for the same offence to be twice put in jeopardy of life or limb; nor shall be compelled in any Criminal Case to be a witness against himself, nor be deprived of life, liberty, or property, without due process of law; nor shall private property be taken for public use, without just compensation.

Article VI

In all criminal prosecutions,-the accused shall enjoy the right to a speedy and public trial, by an impartial jury of the State and district wherein the crime shall have been committed, which district shall have been previously ascertained by law, and to be informed of the nature and cause of the accusation; to be confronted with the witnesses against him; to have compulsory process for obtaining Witnesses in his favor, and to have the Assistance of Counsel for his defence.

Article VII

In Suits at common law, where the value in controversy shall exceed twenty dollars, the right of trial by jury shall be preserved, and no fact tried by a jury shall be otherwise re-examined in any Court of the United States, than according to the rules of the common law.

Article VIII

Excessive bail shall not be required, nor excessive fines imposed, nor cruel and unusual punishments inflicted.

Article IX

The enumeration in the Constitution, of certain rights, shall not be construed to deny or disparage others retained by the people.

Article X

The powers not delegated to the United States by the Constitution, nor prohibited by it to the States, are reserved to the States respectively, or to the people.

Figure 17: Photo Courtesy of National Archives - archives.gov

Article III establishes the judicial branch. It is the branch of government that reviews and explains laws, resolves disputes, and decides if a law is in line with the Constitution.

This branch is considered not democratic, as federal judges are nominated by the president and confirmed by the Senate. The people do not have a direct say. All federal court judges are appointed for life to ensure they are independent of politics and political influence.

Article III discusses the federal court system and the U.S. Supreme Court, but there are state court systems, as well.

The legislative branch of the U.S. government makes laws. The executive branch carries out the laws, and the judicial branch explains the laws. After Congress has passed a law and the president has enforced it, if there is great need for clarity on the law or doubt about whether it is in line with the Constitution, the Supreme Court may examine the law and rule on it.

SECTION 1

Article III establishes the federal court system. The first section creates the U.S. Supreme Court as the federal system's highest court. The Supreme Court has final say on matters of federal law that come before it.

The Supreme Court is independent and not influenced by changes in other court systems. Justices cannot be fired randomly, and their salaries are fixed. There are nine judges in the Supreme Court, and five are needed to rule on a case.

SECTION 2

The Supreme Court only has jurisdiction over certain cases. For example, the Supreme Court must preside over cases involving two or more state governments, but cannot hear a divorce case. Case subjects that the Supreme Court may hear include:

- The Constitution and federal laws.
- Treaties.
- Laws governing ships.
- Ambassadors, public ministers, the U.S. government itself, citizens of different states, and a state or citizen versus a foreign country or citizen.

The above cases fall under original jurisdiction. This means the Supreme Court hears the cases for the first time.

Under appellate jurisdiction, the Supreme Court can hear a case once it has moved through the whole court system, from the district court to the appeals court, and the state supreme court. Only after all lower courts have responded can the case go on to the Supreme

Court. The Supreme Court can hear a case on appeal on almost any subject that involves a point of constitutional or federal law.

The Supreme Court chooses which cases to accept. Lawyers must submit a Writ of Certiorari to the Supreme Court. The nine justices then vote and can reject hearing a case based on either the possible impact of the case on society or simply because they have too many cases already underway.

SECTION 3

Section 3 of Article III defines treason as making war against the U.S. and aiding the country's enemies. You can only be convicted of treason if you confess in open court or if at least two witnesses can confirm the act.

Article IV of the U.S. Constitution

This article describes relationships between states. In some areas, the federal government has direct control over state policy. States are accountable to the federal government but have their own powers and independence on some issues.

SECTION 1

Under the Articles of Confederation, states sometimes mistreated each other and acted individually on many issues. It was like having thirteen small countries close to each other, each doing their own thing.

Under Section 1, Article IV, states must recognize the validity of each other's laws and judicial practices. They must acknowledge official state documentation, such as driver's licenses, which can differ from state to state. A couple married in Florida, for example, will still be considered married in Arizona.

SECTION 2

States are not allowed to discriminate against people from another state.

If someone commits a crime and the perpetrator flees to another state, they will be taken back for trial to the state where they committed the crime.

The Fugitive Slave Clause of Section 2 says that states have to respect the claims of slaveowners to reclaim slaves that flee to another state. The clause is no longer in use today, as slavery was prohibited with the passage of the Thirteenth Amendment.

SECTION 3

This section discusses how new states can be admitted to the Union. It also mentions the importance of respecting the territory of each state. No new state can be formed within an existing state, and states cannot merge unless both the involved states and Congress consent.

SECTION 4

Every state will have a representative democracy. The people select who they want to govern the state, and each state will derive its power from its people and not from a monarchy.

The federal government will protect states against outside invasions and domestic upheavals because the states will no longer have individual militaries.

Article V of the U.S. Constitution

The drafters of the U.S. Constitution understood that the conditions about which they wrote and the decisions they made might change over time. Therefore, there had to be a provision in the Constitution to change the text. Article V sets out the procedure and the different ways people can amend the Constitution.

WAYS TO CHANGE THE CONSTITUTION

There are two ways to propose making a change to the Constitution: a two-thirds affirmative vote in both houses of Congress, or legislatures of two-thirds of all states call for a convention to propose amendments.

Changes must be approved by three-fourths of all state legislatures or special state conventions to become official. The process is lengthy, to ensure that constitutional changes are not made in haste.

Since the Constitution was adopted in 1787, it has been amended twenty-seven times.

HOW OFTEN DO AMENDMENTS HAPPEN?

The first twelve amendments to the Constitution (including the Bill of Rights) were made before 1804. After that, there were no amendments for more than fifty years. After the Civil War, the Thirteenth, Fourteenth, and Fifteenth Amendments followed. These had to do with outlawing slavery, protecting civil rights, and forbidding racial discrimination in voting, respectively.

Another forty years passed before Amendments Sixteen through Nineteen followed between 1913 and 1920. Several more amendments followed between 1920 and 1971. Since 1971, however, no additional modifications have been proposed.

Amendment Twenty-Seven to the U.S. Constitution was proposed in 1789, together with the Bill of Rights. A few states ratified it at the time, but then it was mostly forgotten.

Because Article V does not include a time limit on ratification, more and more states slowly ratified this amendment over the years until, finally, in 1992, more than two hundred years after the process began, ratifications reached three-quarters of all states and the amendment passed.

Because of this, Congress then specified that an amendment must be ratified within seven years or it would lapse.

Article VI of the U.S. Constitution

The Constitution's drafters wanted to guarantee that the United States would still accept all debts and contracts that the Articles of Confederation had entered into. Article IV does this and makes the treaties and laws of the U.S. as the country's supreme law. This is called the Supremacy Clause. State laws are inferior to federal law, unless prohibited by the Constitution itself.

Article VI requires all members of federal and state legislatures, officers, executives, and judges to swear to support the Constitution. Everyone can hold office, regardless of their religious beliefs.

The Supremacy Clause The Supremacy Clause was debated and went through various changes, but the final version states:

> *This Constitution, and the Laws of the United States which shall be made in Pursuance thereof; and all Treaties made, or which shall be made, under the Authority of the United States, shall be the supreme Law of the Land; and the Judges in every State shall be bound thereby, any Thing in the Constitution or Laws of any State to the Contrary notwithstanding.*

This means that the Constitution and its federal laws are the highest authority in the United States. All judges in every state are bound to it, even if their state laws say differently.

For example, if Georgia passed a law to allow the state to print its own money, the law would be void because the Constitution states that only Congress can coin and print money.

THE NO RELIGIOUS TEST CLAUSE

Article VI states that:

> *No Religious Test shall ever be required as a Qualification to any Office or public Trust under the United States.*

Prior to enacting the Constitution, many states in the U.S. required government officials to be non-Catholic Christians, and they barred certain people (often Catholics or non-Christians) from holding office.

With this clause, anyone can hold a government position regardless of religious affiliation. With religious freedom, less politically powerful faiths, and atheists are protected against discrimination.

Article VII of the U.S. Constitution

BACKGROUND

Applying to the time it was written, the final article of the Constitution discusses how states must approve the Constitution. The new Constitution would not have been effective if the majority of people had not thrown their weight behind it. So, out of the original thirteen states in the U.S., nine had to accept the new Constitution before it could go into effect.

State-wide conventions were set up at the time so the people of each state could debate the new Constitution. Some states approved it quickly; others took longer. The whole process took three years. Rhode Island was the last state to support the Constitution, in 1790.

THE DEBATE

There were two sides to the debate about whether or not to adopt the Constitution.

Federalists supported the Constitution, and Anti-Federalists did not. Anti-Federalists wanted to know if the Constitution would protect individual rights and state sovereignty. Would the federal government be too powerful? Federalists said that the separation of powers set out in the Constitution would prevent this abuse, and the Constitution protected individual rights, although it did not explicitly list them.

The debate resulted in drafting the Bill of Rights to address concerns for the individual, and it was added to the Constitution in 1791.

Fun Facts About the U.S. Constitution

When the U.S. Constitution was signed, there were just over 4 million people in the United States. The nation's largest city was Philadelphia, where 40,000 people lived. Today, the U.S. population is more than 340 million.

The U.S. Constitution is sometimes also referred to as a bundle of compromises.

The U.S. Constitution is the shortest and the oldest in the world. In contrast, the Constitution of India has over 390 articles and has been amended ninety-four times. Not that the Americans did not try! Congress has presided over more than 11,000 possible amendments since the Constitution's ratification over the years. Still, only twenty-seven got final approval.

The Founding Fathers debated how to address the president. Some wanted to call him His Highness, the president, but the House of Representatives and the Senate eventually decided to use only the term president of the United States.

The Constitution has three Latin phrases: pro tempore, ex post facto, and habeas corpus.

Jacob Shallus, a Pennsylvania General Assembly clerk, had to physically write down the Constitution on parchment paper so that the delegates could sign it. He probably wrote down the 4,000 words of text in one day, September 16, 1787. Shallus was paid the equivalent of about $800 in today's money for his services.

The Constitution has a few unusual spellings. The most glaring is "Pensylvania" (with only one "n") just above the signatures of the Founding Fathers. The word "choose" is also spelled "chuse" several times.

Benjamin Franklin was known as the Sage of the Constitutional Convention, and he often counseled and acted as a mediator. He was over eighty-years old and in constant pain because of gout and bladder stones. Benjamin Franklin needed help when he had to sign the Constitution, and tears streamed down his face as he signed.

At first, George Washington did not want to attend the Constitutional Convention. He thought it would be a waste of time and would fail. Ironically, he became the first American president on April 30, 1789.

The Constitution created a republic, not a democracy. The difference is that a republic is a government by the people with checks and balances, whereas in a democracy, the majority rules. Therefore, the word "democracy" does not appear anywhere in the Constitution.

The original Constitution is kept in the National Archives Building in Washington, D.C. The document (together with the Declaration of Independence and the Bill of Rights) is kept in a fifty-ton steel and concrete vault. The three papers are each in their own helium-filled glass case, and the cases are raised each morning out of the vault and lowered again at night. The documents are kept at a constant temperature of about 66.2°F (19°C) and a humidity of 25%. The papers must also be protected from ultra-violet light, as it can be especially damaging to the fragile parchment.

A DETAILED LOOK AT THE BILL OF RIGHTS

The First Amendment

This amendment protects the public's right to freedom of religion, to assembly, to address the government, and to speak freely.

The right to freedom of speech and press freedom includes written and unwritten expressions, such as advertisements and art. Therefore, individuals and the media alike are free to express their opinions and views, even if it means criticizing leaders and having unpopular opinions.

The right to freedom of religion means that Americans may choose their religion or even choose not to be religious. The government may not favor any religion above the other. A person may exercise his/her religious beliefs, even if it means wearing certain specified clothing, attending services, or praying in public at certain intervals.

The right to freedom of peaceable assembly and the right to petition the government means an individual has the right to gather with a group of people to protest for political, religious, or any other purposes.

The right not to associate means the government may not force a citizen to participate in specific actions or petitions.

The Pentagon Papers

One of the most frequently cited and significant First Amendment cases is *New York Times Co. v. United States, 403 U.S. 713* (1971) often referred to as the "Pentagon Papers" case.

In this case, the U.S. government attempted to prevent *The New York Times* and *The Washington Post* from publishing classified documents (known as the Pentagon Papers) that revealed sensitive information about the U.S. government's decision-making in relation to the Vietnam War. The government argued that publishing the documents would harm national security.

The Supreme Court's decision in this case was a landmark victory for freedom of the press. In a 6–3 decision, the Court ruled that the government's efforts to prevent the publication of the Pentagon Papers were an unconstitutional prior restraint on freedom of the press. This case established an important precedent that government censorship of the press is highly discouraged under the First Amendment and should only be allowed in the most exceptional circumstances.

The Pentagon Papers case highlighted the importance of a free press in ensuring a transparent and accountable government. It reaffirmed the principle that the First Amendment provides strong protections for the publication of information of public interest, even if it might be embarrassing or uncomfortable for the government. This case is often cited in discussions about freedom of the press and the limits of government intervention in matters of free expression.

The Second Amendment

> *A well-regulated Militia, being necessary to the security of a free State, the right of the people to keep and bear Arms, shall not be infringed.*

The meaning of this amendment has been debated for a long time. At the time of the American Revolutionary War, militias were groups of able-bodied citizens who protected towns, colonies, and states.

Anti-gun supporters advocate a narrow, states-right understanding of the amendment. They argue that the amendment confers a right on state governments to establish militia and that the right to keep and bear arms is militia related. According to this view, an ordinary citizen is not covered by the amendment since this is a collective and not an individual right.

Pro-gun supporters argue that the amendment protects the right of every person to have weapons for self-protection, making it an individual right.

This argument was resolved in *District of Columbia v. Heller (2008)*. In a 5–4 decision issued on June 26, the Supreme Court affirmed the appellate court's ruling and endorsed the individual-right interpretation of the Second Amendment. Writing for the majority, Justice Antonin Scalia stated that the operative clause "the right of the people to keep and bear Arms, shall not be infringed" protects an individual right rooted in English common law and reflected in the English Bill of Rights of 1689.

The majority five judges of this highly controversial case held that the Second Amendment's preamble, *A well-regulated Militia, being necessary to the security of a free State*, is consistent with this interpretation when understood in light of the framers' belief that the most effective way to destroy a citizens' militia was to disarm the citizens.

The Third Amendment

This amendment prevents quartering soldiers in private homes. This protects the individual so that they are not to be forced to house or provide lodging to soldiers.

The Fourth Amendment

This amendment says that citizens are protected against unreasonable searches and seizures of their private property, and that these rights may not be violated.

To convict a person of a crime, evidence is needed. The best way to find evidence is at the person's home or on his person. Prior to enacting the Constitution, there was no protection against the police or government invading a home at any time. The Fourth Amendment says that people have the right to insist on a warrant based on probable cause if the government wants to search their house. The place to be searched or the property confiscated must be described precisely. Any unreasonable searches are outlawed.

The Fifth Amendment

The Fifth Amendment aims to prevent the government from corrupt legal proceedings.

The right to a grand jury ensures that correct and fair methods are used in criminal proceedings.

Protection against double jeopardy means that an individual may not be prosecuted for the same crime twice after being acquitted, convicted, or serving a sentence.

Protection against self-incrimination means that the individual may

> *remain silent and not say anything that may subject him or her to criminal proceedings. A person may even choose not to be a witness in his or her own trial, and this may not be used against them.*

The right to due process of law means that the proceedings must be fair and that the individual's rights must be protected at all times. Whatever the U.S. government does, it cannot remove someone's property, liberty, or even life if they do not adhere to the proper steps.

The right that private property may not be taken/seized by the government without just compensation means that the government may take property from an individual if they provide just compensation, and such property acquisition must be in the public's interest.

Miranda Rights

In 1966, Ernesto Miranda was arrested for stealing $8.00 and interrogated by the police for two hours. Nobody told him that he had the right to remain silent or that he could ask for an attorney. He confessed to the police that he had kidnapped and raped a woman in addition to the theft.

Eventually, a court convicted Miranda for the kidnapping and rape based on his confession, and he was sentenced to twenty years in a correctional facility. Appeals followed until the Supreme Court ruled that Miranda's confession was not valid. The Court said people must not be able to convict or incriminate themselves. It is everyone's right, and the police must make sure that safeguards are in place so that it does not happen.

The ruling established five basic things that people must hear when they are arrested:

- They can remain silent if they wish to do so.
- They can ask for an attorney before being questioned.
- The attorney can be present while they are being questioned.
- If they cannot afford an attorney, the court can appoint one.
- The police can use anything you say against you in court.
- These are collectively known as Miranda rights.

For a confession to be admissible in court, a suspect must be given and understand the Miranda warning. It is not enough for a police officer just to read it to someone. Confessions may be ruled inadmissible if someone does not understand English well or has a poor education level.

The Sixth Amendment

The Sixth Amendment protects people who have been accused of a crime. It prevents the abuse of the judicial system by courts. People who appear in court have the following rights:

- *The right to a public trial* protects both the defendant and the public. The defendant is protected in that the proceedings are held in a public court and not in secret. The public is informed as to what happened and what the outcome is.
- *The right to a speedy trial* is considered to be very important. It ensures that the accused are not held in containment for too long between the date of the crime and the court date.
- *The right to be informed of charges* against you means the accused must be informed of the exact nature of the crime with which they are charged.
- *The right to be confronted by a witness* and the right to call a witness makes sure that prosecutors rely not only on statements made by witnesses, but that witnesses can be called to testify and be cross-examined by the defendant's legal team.
- *The right to legal counsel* means every person has the right to legal counsel, whether they can afford it or not. This also contributes to ensuring a fair trial.

The Seventh Amendment

This Amendment provides the right to a trial by jury in *civil* cases, not criminal cases. A jury, composed of randomly selected citizens, helps ensure that legal decisions are fair and based on the judgment of peers rather than solely on a judge.

The Eighth Amendment

Individuals are protected against the following:

- Excessive bail fines. Bail should not be so high that people cannot afford it. Bail promotes good behavior and ensures that the accused stays put.
- Unusual punishment. Extreme measures may not be used as punishment, such as torture, crucifixion, etc.

The Eighth Amendment was based on the English Bill of Rights of 1689 and ensures that those accused of a crime have reasonable bail money. The Eighth Amendment is also called the Excessive Bail Clause. Bail is the amount of money a person must give the court to leave the jail before the trial. Should the person disappear before trial, they forfeit the money, but they can get their money back if they show up on their trial date.

This amendment prohibits the courts from setting bail amounts too high. If people cannot pay, they must stay in jail and cannot prepare adequately for their trial. Furthermore, they cannot provide for their families and are a burden on the state because they must be fed and housed in a correctional facility. However, the bail amount cannot be too small, as it could mean that the person would simply not show up for their trial date.

An additional aspect of the American legal system is that you are presumed to be innocent until proven guilty. A person accused of wrongdoing cannot be kept in jail indefinitely because no guilt for a crime has yet been proven.

An exception is in the case of a particularly heinous crime. Releasing a dangerous person could threaten a community, and in some of these cases, no bail will be set. So, even though a person has a right to bail, receiving bail is subject to what the court decides.

The Ninth Amendment

This amendment states that individual rights and liberties are not limited to the rights listed in the previous eight amendments and that individuals have several other rights that might not have been listed.

The Tenth Amendment

The Tenth Amendment states that powers not explicitly delegated to the government will be delegated to states and the people. This reinforces the separation of powers between central and state governments. For example, education is not mentioned in the Constitution. It is, therefore, the job of states to educate their people. Whatever is not written in the Constitution is the job of the states.

The Founding Fathers did not want the central government to become too powerful, and as much power as possible had to be retained in the local state legislature.

The Eleventh Amendment

The Eleventh Amendment prohibits citizens from one state or foreign countries from suing another state in federal court. It deals with the issue of sovereign immunity and limits the ability of individuals to sue state governments in federal court.

The amendment was intended to protect states from being subject to lawsuits by out-of-state or foreign citizens without their consent. Consent means that a state agrees to or waives sovereign immunity so that it can be sued in federal court.

The Twelfth Amendment

This amendment addresses the procedure for electing the President and Vice President of the United States. It modifies and clarifies aspects of the original process outlined in Article II, Section 1 of the Constitution.

Originally, the Founders created an Electoral College with electors equal to the number of Congress members per state. The candidate with a majority of electoral votes would then become President and the runner-up became Vice President. This arrangement led to problems and was changed by the 12th Amendment in 1804.

Today, there are 538 electors, and a majority of 270 is required to win the presidency. The President and Vice President now run on a joint ticket, rather than the Vice President being simply the second-place finisher.

The Thirteenth Amendment

The Thirteenth Amendment abolished all forms of slavery. In 1863, with the signing of the Emancipation Proclamation, Abraham Lincoln declared that all persons held as slaves were to be set free. However, this was not the case for all the states. The Thirteenth Amendment freed all slaves.

The Fourteenth Amendment

The Fourteenth Amendment makes all citizens equal. It was also a pivotal addition to the Constitution, especially in the aftermath of the American Civil War. It played a crucial role in addressing citizenship and civil rights issues, particularly for formerly enslaved individuals. It also laid the foundation for subsequent civil rights legislation and Supreme Court decisions, as it established the principles of equal protection and due process under the law, which are fundamental to protecting individual rights in the United States.

The main clauses of the Fourteenth Amendment include :

- The Citizenship Clause defines who is a citizen of the United States. It states: "*All persons born or naturalized in the United States, and subject to the jurisdiction thereof, are citizens of the United States and of the State wherein they reside.*" This clause was added to ensure that former slaves and their descendants were recognized as U.S. citizens.
- The Equal Protection Clause mandates that "*no state shall deny to any person within its jurisdiction the equal protection of the laws.*" This clause prohibits states from discriminating against individuals based on race, ethnicity, gender, or other protected characteristics. It has been central to many civil rights cases and Supreme Court decisions.
- The Due Process Clause declares that no state shall deprive any person of life, liberty, or property, without due process of law. It emphasizes the importance of fair legal procedures and the protection of individual rights.
- The Privileges or Immunities Clause states that *"no state shall make or enforce any law which shall abridge the privileges or immunities of citizens of the United States.* It was intended to protect the civil rights of citizens and ensure that states could not infringe upon those rights.
- The Enforcement Clause empowers Congress to enforce the provisions of the Fourteenth Amendment through appropriate legislation. It grants Congress the authority to pass laws to ensure that the rights guaranteed by the amendment are protected and upheld.

The Fifteenth Amendment

This amendment was passed by Congress on February 26, 1869 and it guaranteed that male citizens could not be barred from voting due to race or former enslavement. It gave formerly enslaved Black men the right to vote, but women of all races were still excluded until later, and other voting barriers (poll taxes, literacy tests) persisted until the 20th century. Subsequent amendments – 19th, 24th, 26th – were needed to achieve universal adult suffrage.

The Sixteenth Amendment

Congress can collect federal taxes on income earned. This is regarded as the biggest source of income the government has. Before 1913, the only way the government could make money was through taxes on imports.

The Sixteenth Amendment was proposed in 1909 and ratified in 1913. With income tax, the federal government could now spend money on the military, social welfare, and even the arts. In the 1930s, federal income tax also became an instrument of social policy used to redistribute income.

The Seventeenth Amendment

This amendment states that citizens will directly elect state representatives to the U.S. Senate. This amendment was made to prevent corruption and give citizens more political agency.

The Eighteenth Amendment

During the first two decades of the twentieth century, people began to see drinking as evil and felt that alcoholic beverages should be prohibited. The Eighteenth Amendment banned the making, selling, transportation, and drinking of alcohol. This period, from 1919, was called the Prohibition Era.

The Eighteenth Amendment was repealed using the Twenty-First Amendment.

The Nineteenth Amendment

This amendment meant that the right to vote in federal elections could not be denied on the grounds of gender, giving women the right to vote.

The Fifteenth Amendment had given male African Americans the right to vote about fifty years prior.

The Twentieth Amendment

The Twentieth Amendment stipulates when the president will take office and when his term will commence.

The Twenty-First Amendment

This amendment repealed the Eighteenth Amendment, legalizing the drinking, selling, manufacturing, and consumption of alcohol. The Twenty-First Amendment ended the Prohibition Era. This may have been because of social outcry, lack of enforcement, or from the need to make money.

The Twenty-Second Amendment

This 1951 amendment limited presidents to two elected terms (i.e., no person can be elected President more than twice). Each term lasts a maximum of four years.

The Twenty-Third Amendment

The District of Columbia (D.C.) is a federal district and not a state. Therefore, it has limited electoral privileges, such as having Representatives in the Senate or in the House of Representatives. However, there was a long-standing protest against this, and as a result, the Twenty-Third Amendment was adopted in 1961 and came into effect for the 1964 election. It gave Washington, D.C. three electoral votes in the Electoral College.

The Twenty-Fourth Amendment

This amendment bans poll taxes. In the past, you had to pay a fee to vote. This discouraged poorer citizens from voting.

The Twenty-Fifth Amendment

This amendment created the order of succession and determines in which instances the president will be replaced. If the president dies, resigns, is removed due to impeachment, or becomes impaired, then the vice president will replace them.

When President Kennedy was assassinated in November 1963, people became more aware and concerned about who should take over in an emergency. The Twenty-Fifth Amendment made sure that there was always a vice president. Congress appoints a vice president by a majority vote of both Houses.

This amendment was used in 1973 and 1974 with the resignations of Vice President Agnew and President Nixon. Agnew was replaced in 1973 by Gerald Ford, and when Nixon resigned, Nelson Rockefeller became vice president .

The Twenty-Sixth Amendment

The Twenty-Sixth Amendment provides that all persons aged eighteen and older may officially vote. Voting is one way for Americans to serve their country.

The Twenty-Seventh Amendment

Congress may decide on a pay increase for members, but such an increase will only become effective after Congress holds the next session. This means that congress members will not receive the increased pay until reelection the following year.

★ ★ ★ ★ ★

CONSTITUTIONAL INTERPRETATION: THE OVERTURNING OF *ROE V. WADE*

Although the Constitution is old, new cases regularly require the Supreme Court to interpret how the Constitution applies to new situations or how previous rulings should be updated. This requires a process called judicial review.

The actions of the executive and legislative branches of the government are not forever carved in stone. They are subject to examination and possible nullification by the judiciary. Judicial review means that the Supreme Court can take action when asked to do so to ensure that all the branches of government abide by the Constitution.

The text of the Constitution does not have a specific provision for the power of judicial review. Instead, this is an implied power derived from Article III and Article VI of the Constitution and established in the landmark court decision of *Marbury v. Madison*.

The Supreme Court has the final say on whether the Constitution protects a right or whether the document has been violated.

The Supreme Court

The Supreme Court ensures that each branch of the government recognizes the limits of its own power. It protects civil rights and strikes down laws that violate the Constitution. It sets limits on democratic governments so that the majority cannot pass laws that harm minorities or fundamental values such as freedom of religion, freedom of speech, and the due process of the law.

When deciding whether or not a law is constitutionally valid, some people say that only the original understanding of the language used in the Constitution and the framers of the Constitution's specific intent are important. Others say the core ideals of the Constitution framers were meant to allow the government to function, protect minorities, and safeguard the basic structure of the government against tyranny. Therefore, evolving interpretation within the modern context is necessary.

When interpreting the Constitution for a case, Supreme Court justices have been guided in their decision-making by the following:

- *Textualism:* The plain meaning of how the framers meant the Constitution to be read in the context of the time of ratification. It focuses solely on the text of the document.
- *Original Meaning:* How did most of the population understand the particular part of the Constitution at its founding?.
- *Judicial Precedent:* This is the most common way to understand constitutional meaning. What were the Supreme Court's prior decisions in cases with similar facts? In the future, the same principles, rules, and standards can govern decisions.

- *Pragmatism:* Weighing and balancing the practical consequences and deciding which will be the best outcome.
- *Moral Reasons:* Under this approach, one might argue that there are underlying moral concepts (such as equal protection) in the text of the Constitution and that these must guide interpretation.
- *National Identity:* Judicial reasoning draws from the district character and values of the American national identity to find the Constitution's meaning.
- *Structuralism:* Inferences are drawn from the design of the Constitution (the separation of powers, federalism, etc.).
- *Historical Practices:* Prior decisions are an essential source of constitutional meaning.

Roe v. Wade, 410 U.S. 113 (1973)

A single woman named Norma McCorvey, known in her lawsuit as Jane Roe, became pregnant in 1969 with her third child and wanted an abortion. However, it was illegal in Texas, where she was living.

Lawyers Sarah Weddington and Linda Coffee filed a lawsuit against the local district attorney, Henry Wade, on Norma's behalf, saying that the Texas abortion law was unconstitutional. The judges on a three-judge panel ruled in Norma's favor.

On appeal, the U.S. Supreme Court ruled that, according to the Due Process Clause of the Fourteenth Amendment of the U.S. Constitution, a pregnant woman has a right to privacy and can choose if she wants an abortion. However, the right was not absolute and must be balanced to protect women's health and the baby's life. The Court resolved this problem by saying that abortions could not be prohibited during the first three months of pregnancy but that there are conditions for the second and third trimesters.

Because of this ruling, abortion was characterized as a fundamental constitutional right, and, in a larger sense, *Roe v. Wade* affirmed the broader constitutional privacy right concerning personal reproductive decisions, a principle that originated with contraception cases. This landmark court decision struck down many state and federal abortion laws and reshaped Americans' thoughts about abortion.

Roe v. Wade Overturned (2022)

On June 24, 2022, the constitutional right to an abortion was ended after almost fifty years when the Conservative-dominated Supreme Court overturned *Roe v. Wade*.

The Court upheld a Mississippi law banning abortion after the fifteenth week of pregnancy. The justices also overturned *Roe v. Wade* (1973) and *Planned Parenthood v. Casey* (1992), effectively ruling that abortion is no longer a constitutionally protected right and giving states the power to regulate it. From now on, each state could set its own abortion laws.

Some of the reasons the justices gave for their decision include:

- Textualism and Original meaning: Abortion is not mentioned in the Constitution.
- National Identity: Abortion is not part of America's history and tradition.
- Original meaning: When the Fourteenth Amendment was first adopted, abortion was a crime at all stages of pregnancy in most states.
- Moral Reasons: Abortion is fundamentally different from other decisions related to contraception, marriage, and sexual relations because it involves taking a life.
- States have legitimate interests in regulating abortion, such as preserving prenatal life, protecting moms, preserving the medical profession, and more.

- The reasoning in *Roe v. Wade* was weak and inflamed debate on the abortion issue.
- The issue must be returned to the people so they can decide future legality of the issue via the legislative system.

Why Did the Overturning of Roe v. Wade Happen?

The Supreme Court is composed of nine justices, each serving on the bench for life. During Donald Trump's presidency, vacancies on the court came up, and he appointed three new anti-abortion judges. As a result, the Supreme Court as a whole became more supportive of banning abortion. In considering *Roe v. Wade*, the Supreme Court asked themselves if the precedent in *Roe v. Wade* had been correctly decided and, if it had not been, what they should do.

In the original 1973 decision, the Court said abortion was a fundamental right stemming from individual privacy as the foundation of individual liberty. The proponents of the 1973 decision argued that a woman's right to abortion stems from the notion of liberty, which in turn, was interpreted as the right to privacy, protected by the Due Process Clause of the Fourteenth Amendment, which says that due process should be followed before any right (to life, liberty, or property) can be implicated.

In 2022, the Supreme Court decided the previous ruling was a "flawed decision," and they could not let it stand. Because of the reasons quoted above, the justices concluded that abortion is not an essential component of ordered liberty and, therefore, it is not protected by the Fourteenth Amendment.

Executive Orders

An executive order is a directive from a U.S. president, acting in their capacity as the head of the government's executive branch. It is not legislation and requires no approval from Congress. However, under certain circumstances, an executive order can have the same effect as federal law.

Congress cannot easily overturn such an order, although they might approve subsequent legislation that makes executing such an order difficult. In return, such new legislation is again subject to a presidential veto.

Executive orders are commonly used. President Roosevelt issued over 3,700 orders between 1933 and 1945 as the United States dealt with the Great Depression and the Second World War. President Barack Obama, in contrast, issued just under three hundred executive orders, and, in his first term, President Donald Trump issued 220.

The Constitution does not mention executive orders by name. However, Section 1 of Article II of the Constitution grants the president the authority to issue such order by stating that, "*The executive power shall be vested in a President of the United States of America.*" There are limits to this power. Sections 2 and 3 of the Article II state that the president should "take care" in issuing orders, and they can be removed if not acting in good faith.

Countering the Supreme Court Ruling with an Executive Order

After the Supreme Court overturned *Roe v. Wade*, President Joe Biden signed an executive order in July 2022, directing his health department to expand access to abortion pills, improve birth control coverage, and do everything in its power to protect women seeking to invoke their rights.

The order protects patient privacy and establishes a task force to protect access to reproductive health care. The order also helps with public education and strengthens the legal options available to those seeking and providing abortion services.

Future of Abortion

With the overturning of *Roe v. Wade*, each state can decide their own abortion policies. Voters can make their voices heard in both state legislatures and Congress to secure the type of legislation they want to pass. Future developments on the issue must come via the political system, not the judicial system.

HISTORY OF THE U.S. NATURALIZATION TEST

An abbreviated timeline of the changes during the last few centuries is as follows:

- The first official law about naturalization was passed on March 26, 1790. If you were older than twenty-one and lived in the U.S. for more than two years, you could petition for citizenship in the common law court.
- In 1795, the government extended the time for residency to five years. The person had to prove good moral character and have people who could vouch for them.
- In 1798, the United States was at war with France, and the residency requirement stretched to fourteen years to deter immigrants. However, the conditions proved unpopular and were abolished with the Naturalization Act of 1802, when the residency requirement was returned to five years.

The new act added that immigrants must give three years' notice of intent, swear allegiance to the Constitution, renounce previous citizenships and titles of nobility, and show good moral character.

In 1868, African Americans could gain citizenship with the Constitution's Fourteenth Amendment.

In 1906, a new act to provide more uniform rules for naturalization was established. Now, for the first time, knowledge of English had become a basic requirement. In addition, judges could ask U.S. history and civics questions, but not much documentation exists about this.

The Immigration Act of 1917 implemented a literacy test, and applicants sixteen and older had to demonstrate basic reading comprehension.

The 1924 Immigration Act, enacted a national origins quota to stem the immigration tide for the first time. The quotas were for 2% of each nationality based on their population numbers in the U.S. in the 1890 Census.

The 1924 act also gave citizenship to Native Americans and established the first border patrol.

The official standard text for the Oath of Allegiance was created in 1929 and stayed unchanged over the next eighty-five years.

The Immigration and Naturalization Service (I.N.S.) was created in 1933 to oversee all immigration matters.

The Nationality Act of 1940 clarified matters and outlined specifications concerning race, ethnicity, residency requirements, and basic verbal English proficiency.

Refugees were added to the mix with the Displaced Persons Act of 1948, which allowed 205,000 refugees over two years. However, the number continued to fluctuate over the next few years.

The Immigration and Naturalization Act of 1952 asked immigrants to demonstrate an understanding of English and a knowledge of some basic American history. The exam was an oral exam.

In 1965, the national origins quota system was abolished,

although the U.S. continued to limit people coming from communist countries during the Cold War. Only close relatives of permanent U.S. citizens and residents could come to the United States.

The Refugee Act of 1980 reduced the worldwide ceiling for immigration to 270,000 and defined exactly who refugees were according to international standards. Under these amendments, there was a regular flow of refugees and emergency admission of people. The law also authorized federal assistance for the resettlement of refugees.

The Immigration Act of 1990 established a new administrative procedure for naturalization and ended court procedures. In a 1994 amendment, applicants with a medical disability could still be granted citizenship if they provided a medical waiver signed by a physician. The exceptions to the English requirement based on age were also amended.

In 1997, the I.N.S. started procedures to standardize the Naturalization Test.

March 1, 2003 marked a new phase in immigration when the U.S. Citizenship and Immigration Services (U.S.C.I.S.) took over the responsibility for the immigration service function of the federal government. The I.N.S. was no more. The civics exam is now a fully standardized, four-part exam that is the same everywhere in the U.S.

★ ★ ★ ★ ★

SELECTED BIBLIOGRAPHY

The following citations list principal original sources and secondary sources that provide key summaries and overviews. Readers are encouraged to consult other online sources to verify their understanding of the histories and potentially differing viewpoints of contributors.

U.S. Civics Test

U.S. Citizenship and Immigration Services. "Civics Questions and Answers (2025 version). Accessed Sept 26, 2025, at https://www.uscis.gov/sites/default/files/document/questions-and-answers/OoC_100_Questions_2008_Civics_Test_V1.pdf.

Questions 1-12: Principles of American Democracy

Britannica. "Federalism." Accessed April 29, 2025, at https://www.britannica.com/topic/federalism.

Core Knowledge Foundation. "Main Ideas Behind the Declaration of Independence." Accessed April 29, 2025, at https://www.coreknowledge.org/wp-content/uploads/2017/08/CKHG-G4-U8-

about-self-rule.pdf.

Emory University. "What the Declaration of Independence Really Means by 'Pursuit of Happiness.'" Accessed May 1, 2025, at https://news.emory.edu/stories/2014/06/er_pursuit_of_happiness/campus.html.

Merriam-Webster. "Republic." Accessed April 30, 2025, at https://www.merriam-webster.com/dictionary/republic.

National Archives. "Declaration of Independence." Accessed April 29, 2025, at https://www.archives.gov/founding-docs/declaration-transcript

——"The Constitution of the United States: A Transcription." Accessed April 29, 2025, https://www.archives.gov/founding-docs/constitution-transcript.

National Constitution Center. "Amendments to the Constitution of the United States." Accessed May 1, 2025 at https://constitutioncenter.org/the-constitution/amendments.

U.S. Government Publishing Office (GPO). "Articles of Confederation." Accessed May 1, 2025, at https://www.govinfo.gov/content/pkg/SMAN-107/pdf/SMAN-107-pg935.pdf.

Wikipedia. "Capitalism." Accessed May 1, 2025, at https://en.wikipedia.org/wiki/Capitalism.

—— "Criticism of Capitalism." Accessed May 1, 2025, at https://en.wikipedia.org/wiki/Criticism_of_capitalism.

—— "Life, Liberty, and the Pursuit of Happiness." Accessed May 1, 2025, at https://en.wikipedia.org/wiki/Life,_Liberty_and_the_pursuit_of_Happiness

—— "Rule of Law." Accessed May 1, 2025, https://en.wikipedia.org/wiki/Rule_of_law.

—— "Social Contract." Accessed May 1, 2025, at https://en.wikipedia.org/wiki/Social_contract.

—— "Trump v. United States (2024)." Accessed May 1, 2025, at https://en.wikipedia.org/wiki/Trump_v._United_States_(2024).

Questions 13-47: System of Government

CBS News. "How Much is the Vice President Paid?" Accessed May 5, 2025, at https://www.cbsnews.com/news/how-much-is-the-vice president -paid/.

Overseas Vote Foundation. "Why is Election Day in the United States of America on Tuesday?" Accessed May 5, 2025, at https://www.overseasvotefoundation.org/post/why-election-day-united-states-america-tuesday.

Plural Policy. "Federalism: Balancing State vs. Federal Powers." Accessed Jan 2025, at https://pluralpolicy.com/blog/state-vs-federal-powers/.

UC Santa Barbara. "The American Presidency Project: Presidential Vetoes." Accessed May 5, 2025, at https://www.presidency.ucsb.edu/statistics/data/Presidential-vetoes.

U.S. Capitol – Visitor Center. "The House of Representatives and Senate: What's the Difference?" Accessed May 1 2025, at https://www.visitthecapitol.gov/sites/default/files/documents/resources-and-activities/CVC_EED_StudentEssay_HouseSenate.pdf.

U.S. Congress, Constitution Annotated. "ArtII.S2.C1.1.11 Presidential Power and Commander in Chief Clause." Accessed May 1, 2025, at https://constitution.congress.gov/browse/essay/artII-S2-C1-1-11/ALDE_00013473.

U.S.A. Government. "Branches of the U.S. government." Accessed May 1, 2025, at https://www.usa.gov/branches-of-government.

Wikipedia. "Election Day (United States)." Accessed May 5, 2025, at https://en.wikipedia.org/wiki/Election_Day_(United_States).

—— "Enumerated Powers." Accessed May 5, 2025, at https://en.wikipedia.org/wiki/Enumerated_powers (United States).

—— "Federal Government of the United States." Accessed May, 5, 2025, at https://en.wikipedia.org/wiki/Federal_government_of_the_United_States.

—— "Political Parties in the United States." Accessed May 5, 2025, at https://en.wikipedia.org/wiki/Political_parties_in_the_United_States.

—— "President of the United States." Accessed May 5, 2025, athttps://en.wikipedia.org/wiki/President_of_the_United_States.

—— "Supreme Court of the United States." Accessed May 5, 2025, at https://en.wikipedia.org/wiki/Supreme_Court_of_the_United_States.

—— "United States House of Representatives." Accessed May 5, 2025, at https://en.wikipedia.org/wiki/United_States_House_of_Representatives.

—— "United States Presidential Line of Succession." Accessed May 5 2025, at https://en.wikipedia.org/wiki/United_States_presidential_line_of_succession.

—— "United States Senate." Accessed May 5, 2025, at https://en.wikipedia.org/wiki/United_States_Senate.

World Population Review. "U.S. States – Ranking by Population 2025." Accessed May 1, 2025, at https://worldpopulationreview.com/states.

Questions 48-57: Rights and Responsibilities

All in Together (AIT). "Volunteering on a Campaign: How to Make a Difference in an Election Cycle." Accessed May 5, 2025, at https://aitogether.org/volunteering-on-a-campaign/.

American Library Association. "First Amendment and Censorship." Accessed May 2, 2025, at https://www.ala.org/advocacy/intfreedom/censorship.

FindLaw. "The Second Amendment Right to Keep and Bear Arms." Accessed May 2, 2025, https://constitution.findlaw.com/amendment2.html.

Forbes. "The 100 Largest U.S. Charities." Accessed May 2, 2025, at https://www.forbes.com/top-charities/list/.

IRS. "When to File." Accessed May 2, 2025, at https://www.irs.gov/filing/individuals/when-to-file.

Law Insider. "Civic Group Definition." Accessed May 2, 2025, at https://www.lawinsider.com/dictionary/civic-group.

U.S.A Government. "Voting Rights Law and Constitutional Amendments." Accessed May 2, 2025, at https://www.usa.gov/voting-rights.

—— "Who Can and Cannot Vote." Accessed May 2, 2025, at https://www.usa.gov/who-can-vote.

USCIS. "Participating in a Democracy." Accessed Jan 2025, https://www.uscis.gov/sites/default/files/document/lesson-plans/Intermediate_RightsandResponsibilities_handouts.pdf.

Wikipedia. "Gun Violence in the United States." Accessed May 2, 2025, at https://en.wikipedia.org/wiki/Gun_violence_in_the_United_States.

—— "Oath of Allegiance." Accessed May 2, 2025, at https://en.wikipedia.org/wiki/Oath_of_Allegiance (United States).

—— "Right to Petition in the United States." Accessed May 2, 2025, at https://en.wikipedia.org/wiki/Right_to_petition_in_the_United_States.

—— "Selective Service System." Accessed May 2, 2025, at https://en.wikipedia.org/wiki/Selective_Service_System.

—— "Twenty-Sixth Amendment to the United States Constitution." Accessed May 2, 2025, at https://en.wikipedia.org/wiki/Twenty-Sixth_Amendment_to_the_United_States_Constitution.

Questions 58-70: Colonial Period and Independence

American Battlefield Trust. "10 Facts: What Everyone Should Know About the Civil War." Accessed April 29, 2025, at https://www.battlefields.org/learn/articles/10-facts-what-everyone-should-know-about-civil-war.

Britannica. "Intolerable Acts." Accessed May 5, 2025, https://www.britannica.com/event/Intolerable-Acts.

History. "Townshend Acts." Accessed May 5, 2025, at https://www.history.com/topics/american-revolution/townshend-acts.

National Parks Service. "A Short History of Jamestpown." Accessed June 25, 2025, at https://www.nps.gov/jame/learn/historyculture/a-short-history-of-jamestown.html.

Wikipedia. "American Revolutionary War." Accessed May 5, 2025, at https://en.wikipedia.org/wiki/American_Revolutionary_War.

—— "Battles of Saratoga." Accessed May 5, 2025, at https://en.wikipedia.org/wiki/Battles_of_Saratoga.

—— "Confederation Period." Accessed May 5, 2025, https://en.wikipedia.org/wiki/Confederation_period.

—— "Constitutional Convention." Accessed May 5, 2025, at https://en.wikipedia.org/wiki/Constitutional_Convention_(United_States).

—— "George Washington." Accessed May 5, 2025, at https://en.wikipedia.org/wiki/George_Washington.

—— "George Washington's Crossing of the Delaware River." Accessed May 5, 2025, at https://en.wikipedia.org/wiki/George_Washington%27s_crossing_of_the_Delaware_River.

—— "John Jay." Accessed May 5, 2025, at https://en.wikipedia.org/wiki/John_Jay.

—— "Siege of Yorktown." Accessed May 5, 2025, at https://en.wikipedia.org/wiki/Siege_of_Yorktown.

—— "Slavery in the United States." Accessed May 5, 2025, at https://en.wikipedia.org/wiki/Slavery_in_the_United_States.

—— "Stamp Act 176." Accessed May 5, 2025, at https://en.wikipedia.org/wiki/Stamp_Act_1765.

—— "Sugar Act." Accessed May 5, 2025, at https://en.wikipedia.org/wiki/Sugar_Act.

—— "Thirteen Colonies." Accessed May 5, 2025, at https://en.wikipedia.org/wiki/Thirteen_Colonies.

—— "Thomas Jefferson." Accessed May 5, 2025, at https://en.wikipedia.org/wiki/Thomas_Jefferson

—— "United Colonies." Accessed May 5, 2025, at https://en.wikipedia.org/wiki/United_Colonies.

—— "Valley Forge." Accessed May 5, 2025, at https://en.wikipedia.org/wiki/Valley_Forge.

Questions 71-77: 1800s

Battlefields. "A Brief Overview of the War of 1812." Accessed May 5, 2025, https://www.battlefields.org/learn/articles/brief-overview-war-1812.

Britannica. "Spanish-American War." Accessed May 5, 2025, at https://www.britannica.com/event/Spanish-American-War.

Smithsonian Magazine. "Today We Celebrate the Time Canada Burned Down the White House." Accessed May 5, 2025, at https://www.smithsonianmag.com/smart-news/today-we-celebrate-the-time-canada-burned-down-the-white-house-127844144/.

Wikipedia. "Abraham Lincoln." Accessed May 5, 2025, at https://en.wikipedia.org/wiki/Abraham_Lincoln.

—— "American Civil War." Accessed May 5, 2025, at https://en.wikipedia.org/wiki/American_Civil_War.

—— "Emancipation Proclamation." Accessed May 5, 2025, at https://en.wikipedia.org/wiki/Emancipation_Proclamation.

—— "Harriet Tubman." Accessed May 5, 2025, at https://en.wikipedia.org/wiki/Harriet_Tubman.

—— "Louisiana Purchase." Accessed May 5, 2025, at https://en.wikipedia.org/wiki/Louisiana_Purchase.

—— "Lucy Stone." Accessed May 5, 2025, at https://en.wikipedia.org/wiki/Lucy_Stone.

—— "Sojourner Truth, Wikipedia." Accessed May 5, 2025, at https://en.wikipedia.org/wiki/Sojourner_Truth.

—— "Susan B. Anthony." Accessed May 5, 2025, at https://en.wikipedia.org/wiki/Susan_B._Anthony.

Questions 78-87: Recent American History

Library and Archives Canada. "First Nations, Inuit and Métis Historical Terminology." Accessed May 5, 2025, at https://library-archives.canada.ca/eng/collection/research-help/indigenous-heritage/Pages/indigenous-terminology.aspx.

The Canadian Encyclopedia. "Indian." Accessed May 5, 2025, at https://www.thecanadianencyclopedia.ca/en/article/indian-term.

The New York Times. "Need a Refresher on the War in Afghanistan? Here Are the Basics." Accessed May 5, 2025, at https://www.nytimes.com/2018/12/21/world/asia/afghanistan-war-explainer.html.

University of Michigan-Dearborn. "How Native Americans Shape the American Experience." Accessed May 5, 2025, at https://umdearborn.edu/news/how-native-americans-shape-american-experience.

University of Vermont. "A History of Tomatoes." Accessed May 5, 2025, at https://www.uvm.edu/news/extension/history-tomatoes.

U.S. Department of Energy. "The History of the Light Bulb." Accessed May 5, 2025, https://www.energy.gov/articles/history-light-bulb.

Wikipedia. "Franklin D. Roosevelt." Accessed May 5, 2025, at https://en.wikipedia.org/wiki/Franklin_D._Roosevelt.

—— "Geronimo." Accessed May 5, 2025, at https://en.wikipedia.org/wiki/Geronimo.

—— "Gulf War." Accessed May 5, 2025, at https://en.wikipedia.org/wiki/Gulf_War.

—— "History of the Potato." Accessed May 5, 2025, at https://en.wikipedia.org/wiki/History_of_the_potato.

—— "Indigenous Peoples." Accessed May 5, 2025, at https://en.wikipedia.org/wiki/Indigenous_peoples.

—— "Indigenous Peoples of the Americas." Accessed May 5, 2025, at https://en.wikipedia.org/wiki/Indigenous_peoples_of_the_Americas.

—— "Iraq War." Accessed May 5, 2025, at https://en.wikipedia.org/wiki/Iraq_War.

—— "Korean War." Accessed May 5, 2025, at https://en.wikipedia.org/wiki/Korean_War.

—— "Lili'uokalani." Accessed May 5, 2025, at https://en.wikipedia.org/wiki/Liliʻuokalani.

—— "Native Americans in the United States." Accessed May 5, 2025, at https://en.wikipedia.org/wiki/Native_Americans_in_the_United_States.

—— "New Deal." Accessed May 5, 2025, at https://en.wikipedia.org/wiki/New_Deal.

—— "Pocahontas." Accessed May 5, 2025, at https://en.wikipedia.org/wiki/Pocahontas.

—— "September 11 Attacks." Accessed May 5, 2025, at https://en.wikipedia.org/wiki/September_11_attacks.

—— "Thomas Edison." Accessed May 5, 2025, at https://en.wikipedia.org/wiki/Thomas_Edison.

—— "Woodrow Wilson." Accessed May 5, 2025, at https://en.wikipedia.org/wiki/Woodrow_Wilson.

—— "World War I." Accessed May 5, 2025, at https://en.wikipedia.org/wiki/World_War_I.

—— "World War II." Accessed May 5, 2025, at https://en.wikipedia.org/wiki/World_War_II.

Questions 88-95: Geography

Washington DC Tours. "Fun Facts About Washington DC." Accessed May 5, 2025, at https://www.trolleytours.com/washington-dc/facts.

Wikipedia. "Mississippi River." Accessed May 5, 2025, https://en.wikipedia.org/wiki/Mississippi_River.

—— "Missouri River." Accessed May 5, 2025, at https://en.wikipedia.org/wiki/Missouri_River.

—— "Statue of Liberty." Accessed May 5, 2025, at https://en.wikipedia.org/wiki/Statue_of_Liberty.

Questions 96-98: Symbols

Wikipedia. "Flag of the United States." Accessed May 2, 2025, at https://en.wikipedia.org/wiki/Flag_of_the_United_States.

—— "The Star-Spangled Banner." Accessed May 2, 2025, at https://en.wikipedia.org/wiki/The_Star-Spangled_Banner.

Questions 99-100: Holidays

Wikipedia. "Christmas." Accessed May 5, 2025, at https://en.wikipedia.org/wiki/Christmas.

—— "Columbus Day." Accessed May 5, 2025, at https://en.wikipedia.org/wiki/Columbus_Day.

—— "Independence Day (United States)." Accessed May 5, 2025, at https://en.wikipedia.org/wiki/Independence_Day_(United_States).

—— "Juneteenth." Accessed May 5, 2025, at https://en.wikipedia.org/wiki/Juneteenth.

—— "Labor Day." Accessed May 5, 2025, at https://en.wikipedia.org/wiki/Labor_Day.

—— "Martin Luthor King Jr Day." Accessed May 5, 2025, at https://en.wikipedia.org/wiki/Martin_Luther_King_Jr._Day.

—— "Memorial Day." Accessed May 5, 2025, at https://en.wikipedia.org/wiki/Memorial_Day.

—— "Presidents' Day." Accessed May 5, 2025, at https://en.wikipedia.org/wiki/Presidents%27_Day.

—— "Thanksgiving." Accessed May 5, 2025, at https://en.wikipedia.org/wiki/Thanksgiving.

—— "Veterans Day." Accessed May 5, 2025, at https://en.wikipedia.org/wiki/Veterans_Day.

A Detailed Look at the U.S. Constitution

Wikipedia. "Constitution of the United States." Accessed May 5, 2025, at https://en.wikipedia.org/wiki/Constitution_of_the_United_States.

A Detailed Look at the Bill of Rights

Wikipedia. "Bill of rights." Accessed May 2, 2025, at https://en.wikipedia.org/wiki/Bill_of_rights.

Constitutional Interpretation: The Overturning of *Roe v. Wade*

Wikipedia. "Roe v. Wade." Accessed May 2, 2025, at https://en.wikipedia.org/wiki/Roe_v._Wade.

History of the U.S. Naturalization Test

Wikipedia. "American Civics Test." Accessed May 2 2025, at https://en.wikipedia.org/wiki/American_Civics_Test.

—— "Origins of the Naturalization Civics Test." Accessed May 2, 2025, https://www.uscis.gov/about-us/our-history/stories-from-the-archives/origins-of-the-naturalization-civics-test.

IMAGE LIST

Figure 1: Photo Courtesy of National Archives - archives.gov
Figure 2: © Shutterstock / Ruslan Lytvyn used under license
Figure 3: © Shutterstock / Ntguilty, used under license
Figure 4: © Shutterstock / Rawpixel.com, used under license
Figure 5: © Shutterstock / VectorMine, used under license
Figure 6: © Shutterstock / Frame Stock Footage, used under license
Figure 7: © Shutterstock / Everett Collection Footage, used under license
Figure 8: © Shutterstock / bigwa11, used under license
Figure 9: © Shutterstock / Ntguilty, used under license
Figure 10: Photo Courtesy of National Archives - archives.gov
Figure 11: © Shutterstock / Everett Collection, used under license
Figure 12: © Shutterstock / zef art, used under license
Figure 13: © Shutterstock / Everett Collection, used under license
Figure 14: © Shutterstock / FStreet, used under license
Figure 15: © Shutterstock / Everett Collection, used under license
Figure 16: © Shutterstock / Buch and Bee, used under license
Figure 17: Photo Courtesy of National Archives - archives.gov

Made in the USA
Monee, IL
25 February 2026

44997645R00125